THE YEARS THAT COUNT

THE
YEARS
THAT
COUNT

*A book that lets
young people think
for themselves*

ROSALIND RINKER

ZONDERVAN PUBLISHING HOUSE
GRAND RAPIDS, MICHIGAN

TO

EVERY YOUNG PERSON

THROUGH WHOM GOD HAS TAUGHT ME

INTRODUCTION

T HE YEARS THAT COUNT" should have been written long ago. I rejoice that my close friend and associate, Rosalind Rinker, has written it. For twelve years as a staff member with Inter-Varsity Christian Fellowship, she has not only learned the basic needs of young people, she has done something about filling these needs. She speaks their language and respects their problems and in her breezy, direct manner, goes straight to the heart of their complex dilemmas, as well as to their individual hearts in this unique book.

In "The Years That Count" (which bridges the so-called unbridgeable gap between high school and college age with an easy, effortless sweep of understanding and honesty), young people, teachers and youth leaders will find the down-to-earth, practical *help* they have been seeking. One glance at the chapter titles and your interest will be aroused. Read each chapter and you will share my unbounded enthusiasm for this amazing book!

If you work with young people, by all means stop pulling your hair and make use of "The Years That Count." If you are a young person in high school, in college, or working at a regular job, read it and begin or continue the great adventure of living through the "years that count" for *you* — also sans hair-pulling. I dare to say also, from having read it through several times myself, that even if you are no longer young, the book can help you compensate for what you may have missed years ago.

With more enthusiasm than I can confine in words, I urge the reading of this book. It *has* to be greatly used of God because it has been written from a very great, Christ-centered heart which aches and longs and laughs with young people.

Rosalind Rinker has done a craftsman-like piece of writing, but more than this, I know her to have drenched each line and each illustration in prayer and love, and through it pours not only her own certainty of Christ, but her personal restlessness and eagerness to see young people "centered down" in the Person of Jesus Christ during the years that *do* count so much.

There is no other book of this kind available. But that's all right, because this one *is*. And it more than meets the urgent need.

EUGENIA PRICE

PREFACE

THIS BOOK WAS WRITTEN with the following persons in mind:

High School Students, who want to get everything possible out of life. To help them begin to think for themselves, and find the answers to life in the Person of Jesus Christ instead of handed-down religious rules or traditions.

College Students, with whom I have spent so much of my life, who should have had many of these questions answered before they went to college. Some of whom are jumping nervously from one "safety-zone" to another, still unable to find a landing place. Consequently they are half-lost with no real purpose, wanting to be someone else, or wanting to be some other place.

Working Young Persons, who feel stymied in their efforts to adjust. To give them confidence that they can meet and cope with their associates in business and industry. To help them see that the Christian life is not necessarily "being different" but can be a means of opening the way for fresh personal relationships.

Beyond this, I sincerely hope that THE YEARS THAT COUNT is written to *all persons,* young and old who are interested in maturity.

ROSALIND RINKER

ACKNOWLEDGMENTS

I want to thank my associate, Eugenia Price, for her initial encouragement to begin this book, and for her love and patience all along the way to its completion. I want to thank Paul Byer, Northwest Regional Director of Inter-Varsity Christian Fellowship, for his real Christian influence on my life. Many of the insights shared in this book I discovered as I worked with him. I also want to thank Lillian Lubbert for her excellent work in typing the manuscript.

R. R.

Chicago, 1958

CONTENTS

THE YEARS THAT COUNT

You and What You Believe

1

HOW IMPORTANT AM I?

How important am I anyway? How do I keep from getting lost in the crowd?"

There is one thing you should know right now.

You are the most important person in the universe. That is, your own universe. Your own world which is built around what you think you are, and what you know you are going to be some day. No doubt about it, you are important.

You are also the most important person in God's whole universe. Yes, you are. Everything in the whole world revolves around you . . . what you want and what you need, because *you are important to Him.*

Maybe you never stopped to think of it like that, but it is true of you, and of all the other "yous" in the world. For the whole world is full of you — you and me. I am the other "you." And what is true of you is true of me.

You are going to meet *me* when you go to college. Who am I? I am just like you. My little world is full of me, and of what I like and when and how I like it.

When "we" meet, two worlds are going to merge *or* crash, depending upon who *you* are. The world is a

17

place where people either keep living in their own little private worlds, or else they move over and let us sit down too, and find that interesting people are all over. And they are all like us. Interested first in *themselves*. This is perfectly natural.

High school makes you aware that you are an *individual*. College can *mature* you as an individual. Maybe it is true that when you are a freshman it seems as though there are thousands of others just like you. But after you've been around awhile, you can spot the students who are known by the rest of the class because of the kind or quality of achievement they have attained: sports, writing, art, drama, grades, or offices held, or personality, or you-name-it. They seem mature. You long to be. You can be.

Maturity can also come to you through that job, no matter how you got it or who got it for you. You may look and feel quite unimportant right now, but gradually things change. And the change is not because your boss has at last found out how important you are. The change will come because in your own heart you know that every little thing you do and say and are, will affect the quality and the kind of work you put out.

You are a person, and you must be true to yourself. You must learn to know yourself. The best way to do this is to learn to know the Lord Jesus Christ as a Person. He's the only One who really knows *you*. Get acquainted with Him, talk with Him, read about Him, discuss Him with others. Soon you will be developing a cooperating partnership, with Christ as the Senior Partner. "Lord, what wilt thou have me to do?" (Acts 9:6, 10, 11). You will begin to know yourself *through Him*.

He would not have you sell yourself short!

Know your capacities, your abilities. Know how much time it takes you to do your studying and to keep up a good grade-point average. If you are not a "brain," then get "C's" to the glory of God, knowing that He has a place for you with your abilities. There is no reason to be ashamed or proud of your I.Q. but there is every reason to be ashamed if you haven't developed its potential.

For instance, you are going to teach. Why not try for high school teaching? or for junior college? or even for a job as professor in a regular college? There are wonderful opportunities today to help students know Jesus Christ if you are a teacher. But this means graduate school, which means good grades, which means learning how to apply yourself to your studies now. The same is true in any Christian or professional field. If you like language study, why not take foreign languages, and keep a high-grade point so you can try for a scholarship and study abroad? Many graduate students today are taking advantage of wonderful opportunities to study abroad, to get acquainted with another country, to be a witness there as a student.

If you have an inferiority complex or a superiority complex, let God level you out. He will "make the rough places smooth."

You are important to God. More important than you are to yourself. You should have some idea of this importance. If you will remember that GOD CARES, that HE IS WITH YOU, and all you do is for His glory, you'll make it, with colors flying. *His* colors!

Yes, You are really important. God is counting on you.

What you *are* during these student years, what you *are* when you walk across that platform and pick up your degree, will measure the amount of real happiness which You will bring to others and to yourself in your lifetime.

Is this important to you?

It is important to God.

2

SHOULD I LIVE FOR NOW
OR FOR THE FUTURE?

I'D REALLY LOVE TO, but I don't have time. I've got stacks of books to read and reports to get in, plus a couple of term-papers, and a mid-term coming up and I just don't have time to mix a lot with the fellows in this dorm." Or, if you're working at a regular job, perhaps you feel your time is all too short. Too many meetings to attend, too much laundry to do, too many errands to run.

Do you call that living? Living means being with people, being friends, letting them know you, getting to know them, finding out what they are like, and sharing Jesus Christ with them. After all, He *is* Life. "In him was life; and the life was the light of men" (John 1:4).

If you are living to get that high grade-point and to be known as one who only has time to "hit the books" you will find yourself minus real friends in a very short while. Now I'm not saying that you should *never* "crack a book," or try to get ahead in your job. Let's not be extremists!

Jesus Christ loves people. If you are where you are because He has put you there (and I assume you will read the chapters on "You and Your Life Work") then He wants to pour His kind of love through you to others. He wants to love the people around you. And He wants to do it through you. Are you ready to give Him time? Or are you always thinking "when I've reached my goal, I'll have more time for Him"? In this case, you are dreaming, and it isn't scriptural to say "dream on!" We are to be "doers of the word."

A girl I know who suffers from this affliction of "living in the future" told me she was called as a missionary to India. I asked her if she had made friends with the girl from India in her dormitory, and she began to give me excuses about "not having time." Living in the future, and ignoring the present! It is so easy to do. I know, I've done it myself.

It does take time to go to that girl's room, that fellow's room. It takes time to go for a walk and a good talk. But even before you make the time, ask yourself this question: Am I being friends just for the sake of being friendly? Or does the other person know I want to talk "religion"? People want *friends*. They know whether you are with them because you like to be or because you think it is your duty. Be congenial for the Lord's sake, not for duty's sake.

Make friends for the same reason Christ did. *Love* with a *motive*. Of course, just making friends isn't enough in the final analysis. There are scores of sincere Christians today who have friends but who can't seem to make the break-over in conversation to begin speaking of their belief in Jesus Christ. It only takes a simple question: "What are your convictions about Jesus Christ?" or "What do you believe about Jesus Christ?" It is seldom easy to ask this question, but with Him it *can* be natural. Then you can enter into a good discussion as to why they believe, or why they don't, and very soon it can be your turn when they ask you, "What do *you* believe about Jesus Christ?"

Why wait until some future date to start to be a *living witness* for Jesus Christ? Why not now? You will never taste the rich fullness of His joy until you begin to share with others and shoulder your responsibility of speaking with your friends about the most important subject in all the world. If *you* don't bring up the subject, who will?

Now there could be a reason why you are burying your head in the sands of "not having time."

How much time are you giving Him each day? What about your daily devotional time? Your *Quiet Time* alone with Him. I believe this has a direct bearing on your attitude toward everything: your studies, your job, your friends, your witness, *your time.*

I find there is a *direct relationship* between my love and my time for others and my love and my time spent with the Lord! Being young is a busy time. And being older is even busier, believe it or not. Just ask any graduate out of college even one year.

There are a few important things which have helped me in my own Quiet Time. And they have to do with *right now,* not the future.

1. *Establish a definite time* and keep it. It seems to me to be right to give the Lord the best, the freshest time of the day, when I can hear His voice, get His direction, talk over the day's work with Him. Give Him at least fifteen minutes as early as you can in the morning. You may have to get up that much earlier. You may be able to find a vacant period when your roommate is at

class. But make it definite. Keep that time carefully, every minute of it. Begin *now*.

2. *Have a definite place.* At your desk, at your bedside, by your trunk. I know two girls in a sorority house who push through the formals hanging in a closet to get to the window at the end, and have their Quiet Times there. I know a boy who goes down to the furnace room for his morning Quiet Time, so he can be alone. Another girl goes into the shower-room in the Phys Ed building when no one is there. You can find a place. When I was a student I found a storage room in the attic where trunks were kept. *That place* will be waiting for you, at *that time,* and the Lord Jesus will be waiting for you too. Find *that time* and *that place* now.

3. *Have a definite plan.* Read consecutively in some book of the Bible. A devotional book[1] can be read at night, but you should read His Word in the morning and let Him speak to you directly through it. Use some notes to help you if you need them on that portion of the Bible.[2] Pray through the events of the day. Write them down. Ask His guidance and help on every item. Pray for your friends by name.

4. *Worship your Lord in Spirit and in Truth.* This is the most essential of the four points. You will find your hymn book and the Psalms very helpful. Worship is being in the presence of the most holy God, and feeling your own sinfulness and inadequacy, and yet adoring Him for His great love. He seeks your worship. "But the hour

[1] *My Utmost for His Highest,* by Oswald Chambers (Dodd-Mead). *Share My Pleasant Stones,* by Eugenia Price (Zondervan). *Streams in the Desert,* by Mrs. C. E. Cowman (Cowman Publications).

[2] *The Berkeley Bible* has excellent footnotes on Christian living (Zondervan). *Search the Scriptures* (through the Bible in five years) (Intervarsity Press).

cometh, and now is, when the true worshipers shall worship the Father in spirit and in truth: for the Father seeketh such to worship him" (John 4:23). Worship will open your heart to the joy which the Person of Jesus Christ Himself can pour into you, and with Him you have all the things you can think of or ask for. You may not be able to realize or recognize "all these things" at first, but all the more reason to seek this realization *alone* with Him. "Seek ye first the kingdom of God and his righteousness; and all these things shall be added unto you" (Matt. 6:33).

Live for today, and tomorrow will take care of itself. Start right now and live as though today were your last day. Love your Lord. Worship Him. Love your fellow-student, and share your faith with him. The joy which comes when the questioning friend becomes the "converted friend" will be your reward for living for today alone, seeking first the kingdom.

3

WHAT DO I BELIEVE ABOUT GOD?

Y OU WILL HAVE TO ANSWER that question sooner or later. I know a fellow who put it off until he was almost through his senior year in college. By that time he had practically convinced himself that he was never sure what he believed anyhow, and besides, he argued, "Can anybody really be sure?"

Right now maybe you think you are fortunate if your parents can send you to a Christian college or high school, or if you are working for a Christian firm, because then you can meet other Christians, and maybe get engaged to one of them. But you will find people everywhere who come from homes where no one ever went to church or Sunday school.

Someone will want to know, someone will ask you, "What do you believe about God?"

Well, what *do* you believe about Him? Are your beliefs personal? Are you really a convinced Christian?

Paul Byer of Inter-Varsity Christian Fellowship asks a question which always makes students think. The question is, "Are you a Christian by persuasion, by association, or by conviction?"

How would you answer that question?

If by *persuasion*, then someone could persuade you

the other way. If by *association,* then as you leave home and high school friends and move on to college or a job and make other friends, you will probably become like them and do what they are doing. To be a Christian by *conviction* means that you have stopped to think. Yes, to *think.* To begin to think about *why* you believe in God, *Who* God is, and to be able to put it into your own words so someone else can understand and know that *you* really believe it.

Most young people know that God has something to do with the Bible, church, and Sunday school, but that was a long time ago, out-of-date, and old-fashioned! Most of them have not read much of the Bible and little of the New Testament. And they cannot understand the King James language very well either. It sounds like Shakespeare. They know a few stories from the Bible and think that is all there is to it. No one they know ever stopped to tell *why* he believes in God, at least he did not express it in everyday language which people can understand. Most people use "church language" and everything is quite vague . . . something about being good, and . . . who wants to be *good?*

"Jesus Christ is the God I worship," said one college student to another, when asked the question, "What do you believe about God?"

Jesus Christ . . . God? Does the Bible teach you that? Why, Jesus was a great teacher, or maybe even the Son of God, but He isn't God! Or is He? Well, what does the Bible say?

In the beginning was the Word, and the Word was with God and the Word was God . . . And the Word was made flesh, and dwelt among us, . . . full of grace and truth . . . grace and truth came by Jesus Christ (John 1:1, 14, 17.)

"And the Word *was* God."

"I used to believe," said Joe Y., "that anything was all right, so long as I 'gave my heart to Jesus' and went to church. Since coming to college, I've had to stop and think through what I really believe, and what the Christian religion really teaches. I'm convinced now, that Christianity *is* a Person, and that Person *is* Jesus Christ, and Jesus Christ is God."

Joe Y. is right. All of Christianity centers around a Person. Not a Person who points *toward* the Truth, but a Person who said, "I AM THE TRUTH." Not a Person who has a vision of God, but a Person who said, "I and my Father are one. He who has seen the Father has seen me."

Jesus Christ and the Father are one and the same.

You never looked at it like that before? Well, lots of people haven't. It might be a good idea to get one of the new translations which make reading by paragraphs so much easier (than by verses) and re-read the four gospels again. God did come to this planet as a Man, and His name was Jesus. He set about quietly, without announcing who He was, to show His power and authority and love, by healing and teaching in a way that astonished everyone who saw and heard Him!

As my friend Eugenia Price says, "What a relief that God turned out to *be* Jesus Christ!"

Many of your friends can ignore the question, "Are you saved?" but the Person of Jesus Christ cannot be ignored. They are tremendously interested in the fact that You believe Jesus Christ *is* God. The God who created the universe. The God who loves them even though they are sinners. The God who is alive now, even though He once died.

"What do I believe about God?"

You will want to be able to tell them in their own language because they do want to know.

And it is a relief and an exciting simplification to get it straight once and for all that Jesus Christ *is* God.[1]

---

[1] For further reading on this subject: *Christianity Is Christ*, by H. Griffith Thomas (Eerdmans). *The Fact of Christ*, by P. Carnegie Simpson (Intervarsity Press). *Your God Is Too Small*, by J. B. Phillips (Macmillan).

4

WHAT DO I BELIEVE ABOUT JESUS CHRIST?

W<small>HAT DO YOU BELIEVE</small> about Jesus Christ?
Jesus Himself asked this question. He was walking with His disciples into the towns of Caesarea Philippi when He asked, "Whom do men say that I am?" (Mark 8:27-31).

It is *the* important question every person must answer for himself. Ask yourself right now: "What do I believe about the Person of Jesus Christ?" Your answer to this question determines your personal relationship to Him. Either you are a believer or an unbeliever. If you are a believer, *what do you believe about Jesus Christ?*

Have you ever spoken to a person your own age who was not a believer, and attempted to tell him what you really believe about the Lord? Was that person interested? Were you *interesting?* Were *you* interested? Did he feel that you were convinced about what you believed? Did you speak of Christ as though He were living, contemporary, *with you,* or as if He were long dead and gone but still quite important?

For a long time I considered that what Christ did on the Cross was the most important part of the Gospel. The fact that sinners can be reconciled to a holy God through the love and the death of our Saviour is certainly the focal point. But in varying ways my attention began to turn toward the Person of the Lord Jesus Christ Himself. I suddenly discovered that HE IS THE GOSPEL. *Jesus Christ Himself is our message.* It began to dawn on me that WHO He is, is why WHAT He did is so important! If He is *not* God in the flesh, then what took place at Calvary is of no eternal value. If He *is* God in the flesh, then the seeming tragedy on Golgotha's hill begins to vibrate with tremendous significance. The reason why the Cross and the Resurrection are important, is because of *the Person* who died on the Cross and who walked out of the tomb! Because of Christ Himself.

When this began to be clear to me, I found I wanted to know more about Him. I began to devour the gospels, when before I had considered these four biographies of Jesus as essential history, necessary background for the Cross, or material for children's stories. I knew them anyway, I reasoned, so for years I had spent most of my time reading the Epistles. But now I was thoroughly enjoying the new things I was discovering about the Lord Jesus Christ. I pored over the new translations. I hit upon the idea of putting myself *right into the very situation with Jesus and the disciples,* and "lived with them" through each situation as it occurred.

What I was looking for was anything that would help me see Jesus as the people saw Him then. His miracles proved His love for individual persons whose lives were twisted and deformed by illness and disease and sin. I seemed to see their amazement, to hear their praises and their questionings. With them, I listened to His teachings in which He claimed for Himself the very character and knowledge and power of His Father-God.

He knew His own identity, who He was, where He came from, where He was going, and why He had come (John 8:14, 13:1, Luke 19:10, Mark 8:31). I began to see that every word and act of Jesus of Nazareth was a *revelation* for those who had eyes to see and ears to hear. God-in-the-flesh was living among men!

Before that time my Christianity had centered on my own experience, or on the "plan of salvation." Now the Holy Spirit was showing me more — He was opening my eyes to see that God-as-man was walking the dusty roads of Palestine, and by all the ways and means at His disposal was showing men and women *Who He really was* (Acts 2:22, 36; John 20:30, 31).

My Bible became a new book. I saw that all of it was about the Person of Jesus Christ. "Christianity is Jesus Christ!" I said aloud one morning.

Then I began to be concerned. How could I pass this knowledge on to young people so that their witness might be *of Him* only? Suddenly I seemed to realize that this is the missing piece of knowledge for which the whole world is looking. If anyone had ever told me I was missing the mark all those years, I would have been offended! But now I saw that every tangle begins to untangle when we *begin* with Jesus Christ as God *Himself* visiting the earth.

Two things I had to find: first, how to help my students discover for themselves who Jesus Christ is. For that personal discovery item is what makes for strong conviction, and strong conviction makes for a powerful personal witness. Second, how to help them express it to others.

I decided on the gospel of Mark[1] as a means of finding out who Jesus Christ is. Why Mark? Because it is short. Only sixteen chapters. Because there is a movement and an excitement and a rhythm in his style that carries one along. Because he wrote about Jesus in action, as people saw Him living through His days on earth, healing a sinful woman here, a leper there, raising a paralyzed man, answering hard questions, or calming a storm.

I wondered as I read all these miracles in Mark, why more people didn't believe in Jesus then, when He was on earth? Paul believed that all the fullness of God was in Him, and that one day every knee would bow and worship Him (Phil. 2:6-11; Col. 1:14-19). And Paul had never seen Him in the flesh! Why didn't more of those who actually saw Him, believe in Him?

Because they didn't know who He was!

Why don't more young people believe in Jesus Christ?

Because they don't know who He is!

Why do we expect people to give themselves to Christ and put their trust in Him merely because we witness to them, or take them to a meeting — when they don't know who He is? It isn't that they have rejected Him. They just don't know that HE IS THE LORD GOD!

Imagine the girl's reaction if a fellow on a blind date turned to her brightly and asked,

"Hey, how about us getting married?"

She would turn to him *un*brightly and say, "Are you crazy? Why I don't even know you! I don't know you at all! All I know is your name!"

She's right. What girl with half a brain will give her

[1] *Who Is This Man?* (Studies in Mark), by R. Rinker.

life away to a man she doesn't know? And what thinking person will give his life away to a God he doesn't know?

Face yourself with these questions now: Is Jesus Christ your Lord and your God? (John 20:26-28) Do you really believe that Jesus Christ is God? The God to be worshiped? Can you sit down with a friend and talk for ten minutes about who Jesus Christ is and how He did His best to show people His identity by what He said and did all the way from turning the water to wine — to walking out of the open tomb? Can you do this without soaring over your friend's head in wide-winged doctrinal explanations? Can you express it simply and clearly? Can you talk about Jesus Christ for who He is — God? Can you convince your friend that you believe in Jesus Christ because you know Him to be who He claimed to be during those years He lived among men?

What do I believe about Jesus Christ?

I believe exactly what was written about Him by His beloved disciple, John (John 1:1-5, 14, 16):

> In the beginning was the Word,
> And the Word was with God,
> And the Word was God.
> The same was in the beginning with God.
> All things were made by Him:
> And without him was not anything made
> That was made.
> In him was life; and
> the life was the light of men.
> And the light shineth in darkness;
> and the darkness comprehended it not.
>
> . . . .
>
> And the Word was made flesh
> And dwelt among us,
> And we beheld his glory

The glory as of the only begotten of the Father,
Full of grace and truth.

. . . .

Grace and truth came by Jesus Christ.

And Jesus Christ Himself said: "I and the Father are *one.*" He did not say I *resemble* my Father, He said: "I and the Father *are* one."

Do you believe Jesus Christ is God?

5

HOW DO I EXPRESS WHAT I BELIEVE?

W HY DOES IT SEEM so difficult to tell someone else about Jesus Christ? We all want to and we all secretly envy the person who can. But just why is it so hard?

It isn't hard at all, if you can get the wrong concepts out of your head and the right ones in. What are the wrong ways? And what are the right ways? Is there any difference between witnessing to a college student and to any other person?

No, there isn't any difference at all. Except that when you witness to a young person your own age, he is twice as interested as he would be if someone older were "preaching at" him. He wants an answer he can understand, and you speak his language.

"But," you say, "why doesn't anyone believe what I tell him? Why does my witness fall flat?"

Well, many times you may think you have witnessed to Jesus Christ, when all you have done is to witness to *yourself*, and you aren't even aware of it. You wonder why your friend has "rejected Jesus Christ" when the truth is, that he doesn't know much about Jesus Christ. What you told him was mostly about yourself, or some vague "church theology" in which he is not interested at all. But he could be vitally interested in Jesus Christ.

Jesus said, "Ye shall be witnesses unto *me*" (Acts 1:8). There are two aspects to a real witness.

First, that inner "living witness" which comes out of the very center of you because you know Jesus Christ yourself. You cannot be around people long without becoming aware that the abundant life of Jesus Christ within you is influencing everything you do and say.

Second, that verbal witness, which is an expression of the Life in you. If you have received Jesus Christ, the Life is there. Your part is to communicate it so that they know WHO is influencing you. "How shall they believe in him of whom they have not heard? and how shall they hear without a preacher?" And "whosoever shall call upon the name of the Lord shall be saved" (Rom. 10:13, 14).

I used to think that verse read, "Whosoever knows the plan of salvation and believes it shall be saved." But it doesn't say that. It says, "Whosoever shall call on *the name of the Lord* shall be saved." It also says that in order to call — people must hear. And hearing means understanding. And to understand I must get it right from someone whom I respect, someone who knows what he is talking about.

People do react to Jesus Christ. That is why you have not really given a witness until you have brought Him into the conversation. They react for Him or against Him. Either is encouraging. Then it is well to ask, "What do *you* think about Jesus Christ?" "*Why* do you think that?" "*Where* did you pick up that idea?" For or against — let your friend talk it out, and then you are on "conversational ground" which is "hearing ground" and there can be endless conversations on the Person of Jesus Christ. Christianity is Christ.

Now let's get back to "wrong ways" to witness. Are there really "wrong ways"? Well, we can modify that, because the Holy Spirit does use many different ways to bring people to Christ. We might as well admit there are ways that seem to offend, ways that do not seem to get across, ways that leave the other person cold and unresponsive. Then immediately we think that we are wrong, that we must have had the wrong approach and we begin to draw back and hesitate to speak to anyone again.

True there are many unwise ways, but the only really wrong way I know is to attempt to witness to Jesus Christ without knowing *Who He really is,* and without *knowing Him.* If we are merely concerned about "giving a witness" because it is our duty, maybe all we will end up doing is to witness to our own experience and our beliefs, when Jesus Christ should be the chief subject of our witness.

"What do you mean, witness to Jesus Christ? How do I do that?"

If you have read the previous chapters on "What do I believe about God?" and "What do I believe about Jesus Christ?" you will already understand what we mean when we say, *know who He is and witness to Him, not yourself.*

There is a time for a personal testimony and the Holy Spirit will guide you to know just when that time has come and will powerfully use it too. But I believe there is a difference between a personal testimony and a witness. And we are talking about witnessing.

You want to be His witness. He wants you to be

His witness. Giving a witness to the Lord Jesus Christ is not inviting a person to a meeting, or telling him not to smoke or not to swear. Giving a witness is engaging in a conversation with someone about the fact that Jesus Christ was God in the flesh, one with the Father, that everything He did and said on this earth was to show us that He is the God who loves us and created us, who died for us, and who is *alive today* and with us always.

I know many people who know something *about* Jesus Christ, but they don't *know* Jesus Christ. And they don't know anyone who really knows Him, and who is convinced about Him. There is a difference between "knowing" and "knowing about." Young people are not indifferent to Jesus Christ. But many of them have been prejudiced through faulty reception and bad broadcasting so that they turn a deaf ear. They don't want to be "preached at" any more. They are searching for thrills and for adventure and for personal happiness.

How can we get their attention? How can we tell them that what they really want to know about is Jesus Christ? How can we reach them?

THROUGH YOU.

You are their friend. They like you. Liking you means winning a hearing. You are their age and you speak their language. Encourage them to talk about their religious background (or the lack of it) and to ask their questions and air their unbelief, knowing that you will meet them on their own level. That is, you will discuss with them, explain and share with them, tell them honestly when you don't know and read the Bible with them to find the answers together.

Now, what have we learned about witnessing to Jesus Christ?

1. A good witness should first know Jesus Christ, so that a "living witness" springs directly from the center of his life.

2. A good witness should seek to be objective and present the Person of Jesus Christ, who He is and what He did.

3. A good witness is not subjective: always talking about himself and his experience. He will back up all he says with conviction and personal experience, but primarily he will be a witness to Jesus Christ.

4. A good witness will first find out what his friend thinks or believes and why he believes that way. He will not cram his own beliefs down his friend's throat.

5. A good witness will learn to speak about Jesus Christ in everyday language, avoiding the use of theological or religious terms which are vague to an unbeliever.

6. A good witness will be one who will do more talking to Christ about his friend, than he will to his friend about Christ. That is, he will spend time praying as well as witnessing.

7. A good witness will be led by the Holy Spirit to follow up or carry through every good beginning.

Be sure to read with him, or to lend him some modern readable translation of the New Testament because it is through the written Word that the *Living Word* is revealed. And remember it is through your conviction of the Living Christ in you, that your witness expresses itself.

6

WILL GOD USE ME?

HI ARDEN!" I GREETED a freshman girl I met recently, and we sat down to talk about the girls in her dorm and what she could do to be a creative witness for Christ.

"Do you believe the Lord can use you this year on campus? In this dorm?" I asked her.

"Well, Ros, I hope He can use me. I know He'll use me if I am fit," was Arden's reply.

"If I am fit, He will use me." Ask me how many times I've heard young people say this as they face some new situation — a new job or a new school year! "If I am fit, He will use me."

What do you mean by "fitness"? Think a moment. You could mean your sense of "feeling right" in His sight because you have not knowingly disobeyed Him. In other words, when your conscience does not accuse you, and you "feel right," then you have *a sense of fitness.* But is that right? Is that really right?

Does God only use people who have a *feeling* of fitness? Who are these people? I'm sure I'm not one of them, because I seldom *feel* fit. Only His great grace and eternal faithfulness keep me usable.

41

"You are not fit for God to use you, you'd better keep quiet," your sub-conscious mind is saying to you. "Look at the mess you make of things! How can you witness to anyone? Better wait until you're doing better." There is an enemy who fills your mind with unbelief every time you will listen, because he is smart enough to play upon your honesty and your failures, and then you begin to agree with him.

It may be true. We do make a mess of things. This is why we need a Great Saviour, and this is why we can tell others about Him, because He is greater than ourselves and He saves us from ourselves. Even though we seem "unfit" He makes us right and clean through His Cross and His Blood shed for us. And He is doing it for us *eternally!* That is, He is continually "making us right" and continually saving us from ourselves, from our sins and from our fears. "Wherefore he is able also to save them to the uttermost that come unto God by him, seeing he ever liveth to make intercession for them" (Heb. 7:25). "But if we walk in the light, as he is in the light, we have fellowship one with another, and the blood of Jesus Christ his Son cleanseth us from all sin" (I John 1:7).

Now let's start over.

"Arden, do you believe the Lord can use you this year on campus?"

"Yes, I believe He can. Especially if I am faithful in my daily Quiet Time."

Well, here we go again. We might as well face a specific problem like this one. Granted that you are not fit, and that it is His faithfulness that you are counting on now — why do you think that is *your* faithfulness in keeping a Quiet Time that makes you usable? Is it your faithfulness that makes Jesus Christ faithful? Of course not, you say, but doesn't my faithfulness in having daily devotions make it possible for Him to use me more?

Use you *more?* Is it quantity we are shifting to now? Let's keep our thinking straight.

The truth is that when you obey Him, the channel is clear, your ears are open, and it becomes a simple matter to trust Him to lead you to the person whose heart has been already prepared by the Holy Spirit. The truth also is that because you are His child, *He will use you as much as He can all the time,* if you will just look away from yourself and what you do or do not do, from your successes or failures, to Himself alone. His faithfulness means, that *He always lives in you,* and even if your faith fails, His faithfulness never fails. "I will never leave thee, nor forsake thee" (Heb. 13:5). "And, lo, I am with you alway, even unto the end of the world" (Matt. 28:20).

His love will reach out continually through you to others, because *He is in you.* His love is so outgoing, that it has to reach out. Because that is what He is like. What you are like doesn't change the Lord Jesus one bit!

I am somewhat of a perfectionist myself, when it comes to wanting to please my Lord, and it grieves me greatly when I knowingly fall short of total obedience. But I have finally faced the impossibility of knowing all the ways in which I unknowingly grieve Him. That caused me to face the fact that I would be in a continual state of self-condemnation over my failure to be "fit" unless I looked to the eternal forgiveness of Jesus Christ, whose very own rightness is given to me, even when I do not deserve it. It is given to me afresh each time I look to Him. But because of what He's like, He gives me "His rightness" every second of every minute of every day even when I am busy with something else and forget to look to Him. That is how faithful He is to us. That is how great His love is for us.

I know that you want to be a witness for your Lord. And He knows it too. You want others to know that your life belongs to Him. You want with all your heart to be able to tell someone else about Him. And He wants you to do this even more than you want to do it.

Just where is the starting point then?

You know now that it is not in a sense of readiness that comes from self-confidence because of what you have done or have not done. The starting point, if you are willing to be used, is *to know that He will use you just as you are.* You are trusting *Him, not yourself.* You are believing that He will bring the right opportunity to speak about Himself to your friends. And He will also make you interested and outgoing if you will agree to let Him. Your attitude of heart is everything. When you really believe He *can* use you, He *will* use you.

Not one of your failures or sins of the past has any power to make you unfit. "Thou wilt cast all their sins into the depths of the sea" (Micah 7:19).

Not any of the worries or fears of the *future* can keep Him from living His life in you. "For I am persuaded that neither death, nor life, nor angels, nor principalities, nor powers, nor things present, nor things to come, nor height, nor depth, nor any other creature, shall be able to separate us from the love of God, which is in Christ Jesus our Lord" (Rom. 8:38, 39). He has told you quietly to follow Him, and just let Him do everything.

"Abide in me, and I in you. As the branch cannot

bear fruit of itself, except it abide in the vine; no more can ye, except ye abide in me. Herein is my Father glorified, that ye bear much fruit" (John 15:4,8). This proves that He wants to use you and it also relieves you of the impossible burden of bearing the fruit alone. He is the Vine. The vine bears the fruit. It uses the branches to hang it on! The vine needs the branches. The branches need the vine.

Think on His need of you. Think on your need of Him. Since you believe that you are in God's will, and that He has given you a life-purpose in serving Him *wherever* you are, will you from this time on, regard yourself as His very own messenger, trusting only in *His faithfulness?*

Will you put that into words and tell Him so right now?

Then, will you put it into action?

HOW DO I MEET THE SCIENTIFIC
ATTITUDE OF UNBELIEF?

By this question you probably mean, "What about the professor or the boss or the head of the department where you are working who does not believe in the Bible and who does believe in evolution?"

Well, you might as well recognize from the start that most of your superiors are better educated than you are. That's why they have the job! You won't be able to change them (they've been like that for quite a few years now) so why not try being polite and respectful as a Christian should be?

Moreover, you need to get a few things straight in your own mind. You *can* come out of that class or office with some clear thoughts of your own so you will not be afraid of "scientific unbelief" again.

Religion and science are two different things. The Bible is not science nor does it attempt to explain scientific things. The Bible is religion, and has to do with God, faith in God, the relationship between God and man, and between man and his fellow-man. The Bible tells us how to worship God, how to pray, how to live and how to die.

The Bible is based on facts from the history of the Jewish race, and facts about the historic Jesus.

Science attempts to explain the physical laws which God has already placed in this universe. This is done by starting with a theory. A theory is a belief that something must be true, because there are certain evidences pointing in that direction. Then by experiment and research scientists come to a knowledge which can be trusted.

A current textbook on *Sociology and Science* gave this definition: "Science is knowledge; and the significance of science lies in the significance of knowledge as compared with beliefs, superstitions and misinformation." We have to remember, however, that all **knowledge** starts with one of those three things, beliefs, superstitions or misinformation, and then is either proved or disproved.

You must also remember that "knowledge" changes, and progresses until what was once "well known to be true" is not true any longer. "Whether there be knowledge, it shall vanish away" (I Cor. 13:8). Look how Albert Einstein changed everything by his theory of relativity, which brought scientists to the knowledge that the atom could be split. Textbooks used fifteen years ago are not much good now for anything but a bonfire. Were scientists "misinformed"? Well, let's say they had "partial knowledge" but they are finding more knowledge all the time. The old knowledge was passing away.

When your professor stands before the class, he teaches his material as if it were the last word on the subject. For example, evolution is not a science. It has never been proved by experience or by actual facts. Evolution is still a theory. And everyone is entitled to hold a theory, especially brilliant men with high degrees whose minds must find an answer for their own existence apart from God. So don't be too disturbed when they assert what they believe as if it were a fact.

Actually your faith in God can become stronger by very contrast to the unbelief in your classroom or your office. Listen to what is being said. Hear out the person who doubts. Learn to distinguish between fact and theory. Ignore side issues or controversial subjects and stick to the main issue of Jesus Christ and His claims.

Ron T. struck up an interesting conversation with Clara B. in such a class, and found she did not know what she believed. After several talks together, he invited her to a week-end retreat held by the Christian Fellowship in that University and halfway through the week-end Clara put her faith in Jesus Christ.

One Monday morning, Mary C., a close friend of mine who really knows Jesus Christ and can transmit His humor as well as His viewpoint, was taking dictation from her bad-tempered lawyer boss in the office where she works.

Her boss stopped dictating suddenly, whirled around in his chair and glared at her.

"You must have had a good week-end, Miss C., you are so infernally pleasant!"

"Yes," answered Mary, "I did."

"Suppose you spent it all in church!"

Mary grinned, "What do you think?"

"Now look here, Miss C.," he growled, "can you honestly listen to me bellow around the office here and believe that I descended from anything but an ape?"

Mary laughed out loud. (The Lord helps her to remain her boss's best audience.)

"What does that have to do with going to church?" she asked.

"Church . . . Jesus Christ . . . Adam and Eve . . . God created heaven and earth! Do you really believe God created *me*, Miss C.?"

Still smiling, my friend replied, "Yes, and I also know how much Jesus Christ loves you."

He snorted, wheeled around in his chair and continued dictating faster than ever. Mary thought the subject was closed but God had other ideas. Late that afternoon just before quitting time, her boss yelled for her to come in.

"Shall I bring my notebook?"

"No, I don't want your notebook, Miss C. All I want you to do is make a very simple telephone call and ask a very simple question. Call up some university or some church and get me the titles of three books on the life of this Jesus Christ of yours . . . not one, *three!*"

Mary was willing to listen to her boss and to let her answer reach his personal need rather than his intellectual need, and she did get his attention by what she said about Jesus Christ.

All of us should be willing to start with some belief about Jesus Christ and then go on to discover more. This is the true "scientific attitude." A willingness also to let others start where they *are* and where they *can*, without confusing them.

No matter what the arguments or questions, we all have areas where we have to say honestly, "I don't know." But what we do believe about God is constantly growing as our knowledge increases through the study of the Bible and through practical living with Christ. You are holding a good "scientific attitude" when you experience God personally through Jesus Christ, and "hear His voice" through the Scriptures, and discover for yourself that your prayers will be answered.

There is a difference between a "scientific attitude" and "science." In both there must be intellectual honesty. While science is objective and deals with *impersonal* knowledge, religion is subjective and deals with your *personal* knowledge of Jesus Christ, for He is the God Christians worship *personally*.

God has given you a mind with which to think and a heart with which to believe, and He will give you friends and books and insight to aid you in keeping a balance of faith and courage in the midst of "scientific unbelief."

"So, as you did accept Christ Jesus as Lord, live in union with Him, rooted and built up in Him and confirmed in the faith, just as you have been taught. And be overflowing with the giving of thanks. Beware of anyone carrying you captive through philosophy and empty deceitfulness along lines of human tradition and the world's elementary principles, and not according to Christ" (Col. 2:6, 7, 8 — Berkeley Version).

You and Your Life Work

8

WHAT IS GOD'S WILL FOR MY LIFE?

T HIS QUESTION SHOULD be thoughtfully considered even before you decide whether you are to go to college or get a job, or before you decide which college you should attend, or which job you should take.

Most young people get jobs or get married whether they go to college or not. The fields of skilled labor, civil service, sales, or merchandising may be for you. Or perhaps the fields of medicine, law or full-time Christian service. Whatever your ultimate choice, there is need for some basic thinking.

"What is God's will for my life?"

Certainly included in that will is your place in the economic world of today. Your own aptitudes, your home circumstances, even the part of the world in which you grew up may have some bearing on whether you will get a job as soon as you are out of high school, or whether you will go on to college.

Why do people go to college or enter technical training or business schools? For a number of reasons. Sometimes these reasons are secondhand, that is, from someone else. I hope you have a personal purpose in considering a college education, a purpose which you can clearly state and which seems worthwhile to you.

Each fall when I visit the campuses and speak to freshmen, I cover three points which seem to include everyone. Think these through with me now and locate yourself and your purpose.

First, *a life-profession.* Everyone needs work to do. People go to college to prepare for a higher-salaried position, a specialized lifetime work. Most of the fellows go to college for this reason and many girls too. This is fine because *you* are tomorrow's leaders of education, government, science and business.

Second, *a life-partner.* It is true that many young people find their lifetime companions in the training school or college they attend. I know a girl who went to college for this specific purpose, and during the first week of orientation she found "her purpose" so she didn't even bother to register at the close of the week! Don't laugh. This is just as important as preparing for and finding a profession. More important, for it is part of your life-work, if you are a girl. In fact, next to being a Christian, the subject of your life-partner is important. ". . . and the two shall become one" in Christ. This is His plan. "For this cause shall a man leave his father and mother, and shall be joined unto his wife, and they two shall be one flesh" (Eph. 5:31).

Third, *a life-philosophy.* This "intellectual" sounding phrase simply means learning how to explain the things that happen to you. It is necessary that you have a life-philosophy. A philosophy that will help explain the things that happen to *you.* That is where Jesus Christ and Christianity come into the picture.

If you are a Christian you will find many of your classmates who are not Christians, but they are open-minded and want to know. College is a time and place to get "squared away" on what you believe about God. You can be a real witness to Jesus Christ there. You can do the same thing if you take a job in an office after high school graduation.

If you are not a Christian, how are you going to explain the tragedies around you, and the disappointments which come to you? Futility and the lack of meaning in life are not strangers to college students. Life becomes cheap and not worth living because there seems to be no reason for being born. That is, if you do not have an adequate life-philosophy.

As a Christian with a living faith in Jesus Christ as your Lord and Saviour even your life-work takes on new meaning. You and God are partners. You are not living for yourself but for Him. If you are not sure which kind of work is best for you, if you are not sure which profession you should follow, ask Jesus Christ. He will guide you if you ask Him.

And without Jesus Christ to make you one with your life-mate, what chances do you have for married happiness? After all, sociology tells us that three out of nine couples are divorced and three of the others want to be, but are not only because of the children! That means you have only one out of three chances for lasting happiness in your marriage, unless you take Jesus Christ with you into it. We'll talk more about this in a later chapter.

For *now*, should you go to college?

During the writing of this book, I have spoken with a young woman who graduated from high school six years ago. The question of college or a job faced her. She was not particularly interested in college, and after she prayed about it, she went to a short-term business school and became a secretary. College seemed just out-of-the-picture for her and she was perfectly happy where she was. God had led her and she knew it. Then she got a job as secretary in a large church near a state university. New influences began to reach into her life.

She had been working at this job about a year when I met her. During the course of our conversation she told me she was entering college the next fall. I asked why. Here is her reply.

"I'm going to college because I feel it is God's will for me. I didn't feel that way when I finished high school and I know He led me then. I'm sure that with the experience I've had and the maturity I've gained in the business world, that I'll get more out of college than I would have six years ago. I plan to be a missionary, and I'd like to go out with the Wycliffe Translators. I feel there is great value in a college education — in training, discipline and knowledge. Besides, most mission boards require a college education."

Then I know a fine young man who is a freshman in one of our state colleges. He is not sure where the Lord wants him, nor whether his major will be history or sociology or anthropology. But he doesn't have to declare himself as to his field of study until his freshman requirements are finished. He believes and is sure that by that time he will know, and that his purpose for now is to keep going and get the best possible preparation.

Should you go to college? Should you go directly into a job? "What is my purpose in life?" Write it down, pray about it, talk it over with your parents until there is a quiet conviction in your heart that your decision is right for you. You know the circumstances of your own life and so does God. Together, you can find the best place for you.

9

WHICH COLLEGE SHOULD I ATTEND?

I F YOU HAVE SELECTED your college, ask yourself: why did I choose that particular college?

"Well, you see, my great-grandmother went to Easton when it was still an academy, and my brother went there, and my parents would like to have me go there, too."

"Centerville is where our church college is located, and three of us plan to go there together. We can get scholarships — and jobs, too."

Those are good reasons. Any more?

Oh, it could be that the boy-friend is going to that college, or the girl-friend. Same difference. Good reason. Or, it could be that you live in a college town, and for financial reasons, it seems best for you to attend that college and live at home.

Hugh W. gave me his reason for the college of his choice. "You see, Ros, I plan to be a medical missionary. That means four years of college, four years of pre-med, and two years as an intern. I want the very best, because other countries are particular about degrees. This university has a 'top' reputation abroad. I've prayed about it and feel this is what I should do, and where God wants me."

Which of these has thoughtfully chosen a college?

I wonder if you have discovered what it is that should influence you in choosing a college? Yes, if you have stopped to think about it, you've seen that you need *a real purpose,* not just an excuse.

If you're going to college, what is your purpose in going to college?

Are you going because your parents want you to go? Or because your friends are going? Or because you cannot make up your mind what you want to do yet, so you're going just to be going? Or simply because the college is in your home-town?

This is all good. But it isn't good enough if you are a follower of Jesus Christ. He wants you to consider carefully, to ask for advice and prayer from older people. He wants you to bring yourself and your future to Him, and *pray* until your heart is quiet, and He can speak to you and guide you. He has a purpose for you, and He will tell you what it is. You do need information, though, to help you understand His purpose, and that is what you will find as you read on.

Let's say that you have thought it through, that you do have a purpose. You want to be a nurse? Or an engineer? Or a school teacher?

Then, first of all if you can, go to your parents. Take them into your confidence. Tell them you want to pray about where the Lord wants you to go to college. Ask them to pray for you. Keep them informed and share your thoughts with them as your plans develop.

Your high school principal will help you. Your pastor will help you. Find out which colleges offer a good degree in your field. Some schools are better known for their department in Science, others for Education, or Music, or Home Economics. Be sure you find out about this accurately and as early as possible.

Then there are scholarships. Thousands of dollars are given away yearly in free scholarships. Investigate this, because you could be one of the students who receive a scholarship. Apply for one. Get a job early, too, if you have to work your way through.

This business of choosing a college is an important one. Not only because of your purpose, your training and your profession, but because of two other things I really feel are of equal importance.

The first is the will of God for *you*. Up to this time you have been under the parental roof. Now you will be moving out on your own.

Are you moving in the will of God? Or are you moving because of choices and plans *you* have made? Ella M. was planning on a college degree so she could go abroad and start an orphanage in another country. She thought this was a worthy idea, and of course God would approve. She had not thought of praying over her plans and things were not moving so well. Then she turned her plans over to Him. He did bless them, and after her training was finished, the way was opened for her to do just what her heart desired to do. "Delight thyself also in the Lord; and he shall give thee the desires of thine heart" (Ps. 37:4).

For years I thought God always wanted me to do the hardest thing, the most distasteful thing that I could think of! But now I know He is not like that. He often gives us the desires that He wants to bring to pass in our lives, or changes our desires to become like His. This is part of Redemption.

Please do take your plans to the Lord Jesus. Yes, yes, He does expect us to use our heads! That is why He gave them to us. It is a combination of thinking and of bringing our thoughts to Him. He is waiting for you. He wants you to enjoy His plans and Himself, then you will carry His joy everywhere you go.

Moving in the will of God means you have carefully thought things through. *And prayed.* Have you prayed? I changed my whole program once because someone asked me that question. I had chosen a certain college, had a job there that fall, and everything was set. At a young people's conference that summer I was in a tight place trying to park the car, and a family friend came over to help me. Then he asked, "Rosalind, have you prayed about where you are going to school this fall?" I looked at him a minute and said, "No." That was all, but I went off alone to talk to the Lord. I was seventeen. Little did I know by putting my college plans into His hands then, that in three short years I would be on my way to China as a missionary-secretary! That was because a friend reminded me to pray.

The second reason I feel that choosing your college in God's will is important, is because there you will meet people who can influence your whole life, and become your lifelong friends. One of these may be your future wife or husband.

There on that campus with you will also be the people whom *you* will influence because you are a Christian, and because the Lord has put you there. Marjorie S. is a real believer in Jesus Christ today because Joan L.

prayed about where to go to college and prayed about who should be her roommate. Joe Y. is a leader in a University Christian group today because Roger S. prayed about where he should go to college. There are those who will be ready and waiting for you.

Have you prayed about going to college?

Have you *prayed* about which college you should attend?

10

SHOULD I GO TO A CHRISTIAN COLLEGE OR A SECULAR COLLEGE?

T HIS IS A $64,000.00 QUESTION. Several times I've almost "lost out" because I didn't answer it the way some people thought it ought to be answered. The right or the wrong answer to this question depends on your own background, your viewpoint, *and the will of God for you.*

I hope you have already read the chapter before this one called "Which College Should I Attend?" It is a good idea to begin by knowing your purpose. I believe you will see for yourself that as you read on you will want to examine your purpose more closely to see if it is the right one for you.

Why is it such a hard thing to consider a secular college? Why is it that most Christian girls and fellows go to a Christian college? Maybe you think you aren't interested in reading through this chapter, but I hope you will, because it will not only make you re-examine your own purpose, it will help you to understand why others go to secular colleges.

Christian colleges are wonderful institutions. I went

to one myself. Thousands of pastors, missionaries, teachers and Christian business men have come from Christian colleges. Many young people find there for the first time in their lives that "being a Christian" is normal and respectable, and that there are sharp, good-looking fellows and girls who follow Christ. They learn that Christians, after all, are real people. A Christian college is a great place to get one's roots down, and a great place to find tomorrow's leaders in the Christian churches, as well as in the business world.

In the state colleges and universities are found most of our future bankers, lawyers, doctors and teachers. As freshmen, these people are wide-open to the life-philosophies of their fellow-students, even when they won't go to any church.

Now it may be that *you* should go to a Christian college, but that depends on your background, your purpose and how God leads you. John B. for instance.

"I was converted during my junior year in high school. My home is not a Christian one, and I don't know very much about Jesus Christ. I'm planning to go to a Christian college, and if the Lord wills, I'd like to go to a good seminary too, and be ready to work for Him."

John needs the influence which the atmosphere of a Christian college can give him.

But here is Allen M. His whole background is in Christian schools: He was reared in a Christian home, went to a Christian grammar school, a Christian high school, and is planning to enter a Christian college before seminary and the ministry.

What about Allen? Maybe he needs to develop his Christian backbone a bit, by being with fellows his own age who don't believe what he believes. Some day he will want to reach men for Jesus Christ as a minister. How about starting now?

"Well," someone says, "he might lose his faith and become an agnostic or an atheist."

Strange, but it doesn't seem to work that way. As a counsellor for Christian students in secular universities, I have watched two kinds of "Christian" students come on campus. Those who "lose" their faith in college are mostly those who had no personal convictions when they arrived. They were Christians by "persuasion" or by "association." They really had little to lose. Arriving on campus, they immediately sought friends and campus activities which did not bring them in touch with other believers. Those who came to college with real faith in Jesus Christ, that is those who were "convinced Christians," soon found other students who were believers and together they found the answers to questions that bothered them. The very contrast served to develop maturity and spiritual backbone.

I have been asked on several occasions to speak to the juniors and seniors in Christian high schools. I remember that I once asked three college seniors to go with me to speak for themselves. All three of those girls had come to know and love Jesus Christ in a secular college because other girls had witnessed to them, loved them, and prayed for them. What if those Christian girls had not been in that dormitory? Who would have told these girls about Eternal Life?

Yes, I know I graduated from a Christian college, but since that time I have seen the wonderful witness to Himself that Jesus Christ has raised up on most secular campuses across our land. I have seen hundreds of Chris-

tian students on secular campuses mature into strong
Christians, taking places of responsible leadership in Sunday schools and churches, and after seminary go into
the ministry all over the world. If I were seventeen today
I know I would give careful consideration and pray much
about being a witness to Jesus Christ on a secular campus.
But *not* unless I were *sure* about my own convictions and
knew in my heart that I *would* seek out other believers and
add my witness to theirs.

Here, in the choice between a Christian or a secular
campus, is a fine line of differentiation, and your background and your personal relationship with Jesus Christ
makes the difference! *Pray.* God knows whether He needs
you on a secular campus, or whether *you* need the spiritual
protection of one of our fine Christian colleges. In the next
chapter we are going to look honestly and openly at the
advantages of each. Please study these advantages prayer-
fully.

11

WHAT ARE THE ADVANTAGES OF EACH?

I HOPE YOU HAVE just read the four preceding chapters, because they form a solid background for what you will find in this chapter.

In the chapter, "What Is God's Will For My Life?" we took up the matter of having *a real purpose*. In the chapter, "Which College Should I Attend?" we went into the subject of *the will of God* in choosing a college. Then in the chapter, "Should I Go to a Christian College or a Secular College?" we began to face the challenge of *being a witness to Jesus Christ* on a secular campus, as well as the opportunity for growth and stability on a Christian campus.

No one can make the decision without careful thought and earnest prayer. Each one has to consider these points: (1) his purpose, (2) his own spiritual background, (3) his present needs and (4) his future needs in the light of the will of God for him *personally*.

Before you read carefully the advantages of each kind of college, do read those first four chapters. After you have considered some of these things, if you decide on a Christian college, it might be well to go to a reliable minister or a counsellor who can guide you to a college with a Christ-centered spiritual life and sound Biblical teaching.

Begin to move on the strength of your own convictions in the will of God as the Holy Spirit reveals it to you, and you will find that Jesus Christ has gone before you, and will be with you, for He has promised, "Lo, I am with you alway!"

The will of God does not always come to us with every point crystal-clear, logical and understandable. Sometimes He calls on us to obey and move into action, and then He shows us *why later*. But we are still responsible to consider intelligently all that our decision might entail.

Compare these points carefully from where *you* stand:

ADVANTAGES OF A SECULAR COLLEGE

1. A state degree is usually more acceptable in foreign countries. If you are thinking of serving abroad this is to be considered. If you plan on a professional career, academically the secular university will give you a wider choice of electives. This is, of course, a generality. *There are exceptions.*

2. Laboratories and libraries for research are, as a rule, more extensive in most secular colleges. There are certain fields of study

ADVANTAGES OF A CHRISTIAN COLLEGE

1. If you are planning a professional career, you might take a suggestion from others who have done their undergraduate work at a religious college and then have gone on to a state university for higher degrees. This offers the advantages of a spiritual atmosphere during early years. Please do not be misled. All Christian colleges do not have inferior academic standards. Some rank high scholastically and only admit students with high averages.

2. All planned activities are geared for you as a Christian. Recreational facilities and Christian cultural advantages are on your

such as law, medicine, engineering and physics in which you will need these facilities.

3. Your professors will, in the main, be nominal believers, if not open agnostics, and yet they will be "tops" in their fields. Your powers of thought can be matured as you are forced to think through many subjects, from both a Christian and a non-Christian viewpoint. Classes from these men will also expose fellow-students who are open-minded and thinking, and you can find opportunities to talk to them after class-periods about faith in Jesus Christ.

4. Being on a secular campus can be like a white harvest field, and you will be thrown with all kinds of people in various stages of unbelief, agnosticism, or open-seeking. You can develop some spiritual "muscles" as you learn to think things through for yourself and learn to express yourself in terms others will understand. You will be forced to trust the Lord in a new way to help you live the kind of life which will glorify Him there.

5. You will meet a few Christians there and experience the unique fellowship of those who follow Jesus Christ, regardless of denomination, the particular

side at a Christian college, and you have no major decisions to make. The temptation to compromise your Christian life will definitely be less than on a secular campus.

3. Your professors are believers, and will teach all subjects from a Christian viewpoint. You will most likely not be exposed to "scientific unbelief" in your classrooms. This is also a generality, and depends upon the spiritual standards of the college.

4. The greater majority of students on campus will be Christians, either because of home background or by their own choice. You will find a different atmosphere from that in your local high school and enjoy making friends your own age who believe as you do. You may find your life-partner there. Dating definitely becomes simpler and less complicated.

5. You will meet believers from various churches, and find that one wonderful thing we all have in common is faith in Jesus Christ. You may have dor-

kind of fellowship given to those who seek to make Him known in dark places. At more than 500 secular colleges and universities you will find active Christian groups. Your unity will be found around the Person of Jesus Christ. You will share and pray and work and witness together to win your classmates for Him. You will see many of them considering and accepting Christ, and growing in the knowledge of Him, as a direct answer to your prayers. This in turn will strengthen your own faith.

6. You will meet many international students, some from wealthy and influential homes whom you could never know if you visited their countries. You will find that they want to know about the Christian faith *from you*, their fellow-student, and that they are willing to talk and read and study *with you*. They want friends from the Christian faith who are real believers.

mitory prayer meetings, Bible studies, and discussions which will be very helpful to you as a growing Christian. Even in Christian colleges you will meet a few non-believers or at least "rebels" who are against their parents' religion. This is a good chance for you to let them see Jesus Christ as He is — in you.

6. There will no doubt be international students on a Christian campus, but the probability is that most of them will be Christians. Making friends with them will be a broadening experience for you. Invite them to your home for a week-end or a holiday. They love to visit American homes, and the influence of a Christian family at such times is almost beyond our comprehension.

We have said this before. Here it is again. You are *you*. With your background, your personality, your abilities, your brain, your dreams, your potential, your plans for your future. God knows all this because He created you, and if you are His disciple, He is leading you now in the direction He would have you go.

Your decision between a secular or a sacred college hinges upon all these things which have to do with you.

Above all, evaluate carefully your own relationship to Christ. Depending upon this, you may be helped or hindered on either a secular or a Christian campus.

God will guide you according to His will for you as you *are* right now, and as He alone sees what you will be because you are following Him.

12

WHERE SHOULD I LIVE?

WHY IS IT IMPORTANT where I live?"

"I thought the only question was, whether to live *on* or *off* campus if I go to college. What is there to consider if I take a job?"

Everything is important. Every little thing! Because you are God's child, every single thing is important. And haven't we already said that it is *people* who make the difference? Yes, people. How can people make the difference? you ask. Haven't you heard the old saying, that you become like the people with whom you live? Going to college or taking a steady job changes you, matures you, brings new interests into your life. But the change comes always through the people you meet. The people with whom you work or attend classes. The people with whom you play. Especially the people with whom you live!

If you have already taken a job or are planning to work when you graduate from high school, give much thought to your living conditions. Perhaps you are going to live at home. If so, this requires a new personality development from you. You're a salaried person, or you will be, and this means you are to take your place in society as a responsible citizen. You'll find that there is a "society" to be considered right in the home in which you grew up. You are no longer a child. No longer dependent upon your parents. You have moved into adulthood where those who are truly adult are interdependent. That is, you are to be depended upon as well as being dependent. You are needed by your parents. Not only as a contributing member of your home "society" financially, but in the love and responsibility departments too. Try putting yourself in your parents' place. Identify yourself with them. It is strange to them too that you are now an adult. So don't be surprised if, from habit through the years, they sometimes still try to boss you around. Remember, you are as a Christian what you are at home! Not what you are at a prayer meeting.

Sharing an apartment with other working young people is a possibility for you and this too requires that you remember that you are an adult with responsibilities to share. Mother won't be there to pick up your clothes after you have dropped them. Unless you are a strong Christian, it is not advisable for you to live with unbelievers. If you are allowing Jesus Christ to be Lord in your life, sharing living quarters with unbelievers can be as big an opportunity to witness for Christ as attending college on a secular campus. But be sure of your own convictions first.

If you are planning to take a steady job after graduation from high school, particularly if the job is not in your home-town, consider a YWCA or a YMCA or one of the many "homes away from home" operated by independent and denominational groups. These will give you an opportunity for Christian fellowship and witnessing and also lessen the possibility of acute loneliness which can come to anyone who suddenly finds himself away from familiar surroundings.

Above all, don't put off finding a church home and a group of young people with whom you can share your own experiences with Jesus Christ. On campus or on the big adventure of a new job in a strange city, this is of prime importance. Don't fool around about it. And don't excuse yourself by saying you are a stranger yet and have to learn your way around. God is on your side and it is up to Him to direct you to the right group for you. If you are open to His direction, He will do it.

Now, perhaps you are on your way to college. Where should you live? What does it mean to live on campus or off campus, and what are the possibilities? "On-campus living" means that you live right on the campus, with other students in a dormitory or a house with a House Mother, and are under college regulations. "Off-campus living" usually means living off the campus. For most freshmen it means that the college town is your home town and that you are living right at home and going to college classes and activities.

Let's look at these alternatives more closely so you will understand the real issues back of them.

1. *Off campus.* Students who live at home are usually tied up with family comings and goings, with local friends, local church (that's good!), and with a local job. This sometimes cuts them off from new campus influences (that's bad!). The other day a mother told me that she was praying that it might be possible for her son to live "on campus" for one or two years of his college life, because that way he would be making friends and decisions "on his own." Then he would be learning how to live his own

life because of who he is and what he is like, instead of depending entirely upon home or parental protection. Living away from home you will really find out whether your Christian life and faith are part of *you*, or whether you have just "acquired" it through association.

If your family finances are such that it seems necessary for you to live at home, why not begin to pray that the way will be opened for you, if possible, to live on campus for a year or two of your college life? There are hundreds of young people who live on campus and work their way through college without any help from home. This maturing process makes an interesting adult out of a teenager in no time!

2. *On Campus.* There are three possibilities which you might consider. *It is important where you live.* Scores of young people get into wrong living-units and as a result meet the wrong people and end up with low grades because of time wasted or wrongly spent and eventually drop out of college.

Your Father in heaven is willing to guide you. He has a place just right for you. Ask Him about this. "Therefore I say unto you, What things soever ye desire, when ye pray, believe that ye receive them, and ye shall have them" (Mark 11:24). He loves to have you ask for definite things. You might pray, "Lord, put me into the right living-unit, where I will meet the people You are bringing there — people with whom I can share Jesus Christ — people with whom I can pray and talk and mature — thank You, Lord."

Then you can go into this year's college work with the confidence that you are just where God wants you, in the college of His choice *for you*, in the living-unit of His

choice *for you,* in the classes which will lead to the profession He has planned *for you.*

What are the three "on-campus" living possibilities?

1. College dormitories.
2. Greek houses — sororities or fraternities.
3. Cooperative Houses.

Here we come to a controversial subject and we
might as well face it. I'm not advocating that you join a
Greek society. I fully respect the conviction held by many
of God's people that secret societies are unscriptural. This
is a point you will have to settle for yourself. I am merely
stating that Greek houses *are* on campus and that our Lord
loves these people as much as He loves those who live in
dorms or co-ops. They need Him just as much. It may be
that He will be leading someone to go there. He has done
it in the past and raised up students to be a positive witness to Jesus Christ in many Greek houses on many campuses with definite conversions resulting. I would suggest
counsel with your youth director, your pastor, or someone else whose judgment you respect.

The Greeks and the Independents on campus are
as fanatically loyal as are Democrats and Republicans!
(The Independents are all those who are not members of
Greek societies.) Yet there are people who "change horses
in the middle of the stream" all the time. A Greek girl
moves into a dormitory. An Independent fellow joins a
fraternity.

I met a girl who left her sorority and moved into a
dorm. When I asked her why she did it, she replied,
"More freedom. I want to do as I please when I please,
and not always be governed by the group decision. My
whole life was regulated by what the majority decided.

My dates. My study hours. My dinner companions. My social life. My clothes. My coming and my going, getting up and going to bed. I just want some freedom to make my own decisions and live my own life."

Then there was the Sophomore girl who was being "rushed" by a certain sorority and wanted to talk it over. She knew there would be some difficult places for her as a Christian, but she felt she could be a witness to Jesus Christ among the friends she had already made in that house. And she wasn't too happy in the dormitory. Maybe *she needed* the group-control. Yes, she joined. And it is through girls like Barbara that persons like myself are invited into a Greek house as dinner guests, and afterwards invited to speak about Jesus Christ to the girls in that house. On one such occasion, they asked questions for two hours afterwards. One young woman talked to me alone and put her faith in Christ. The house-mother walked home with me so she could talk about her own needs, and we had prayer together before we said "good-night."

You should consider every angle before you make your final decision. I want to be as impartial as possible in my discussion, because one of these is going to be *right* for you, but you yourself must make the decision. If you let someone else make it for you, you'll be like the girl who went to see the psychiatrist.

"Well, what can I do for you?" he asked.

"All day long, it's the same thing! Decisions, decisions, decisions!" she replied.

"What kind of work are you doing?" he asked.

"Sorting oranges," was her answer.

Well, let's go on "sorting oranges" and take the co-op house next. Hundreds of students would never get through college without co-ops. They are large houses made over into sometimes quite attractive living-units by adding a large sleeping porch with triple deck bunks. Usually there are three or four persons studying in one room. Total number: between 25 and 40. Everyone helps with cleaning, meals and serving, so that living expenses are cut about half. Some of them are far from "plush," but it's a good way to get through college on "shoe-string finances."

Then there is the good old college dormitory. Symbol of American democracy and personal liberty! Sometimes freshmen are put into certain wings or certain dormitories and allowed to choose their own living quarters for the sophomore year. No matter what your home background, everything is equalized here. You get acquainted with a larger number of people, and in turn have a wonderful "harvest field" when it comes to sharing your faith in Jesus Christ or having "bull-sessions." Be sure to read the chapter on "How Do I Express What I Believe?" to know what He has done through other students in college dormitories.

If you are living at the "Y" or in a boarding house of some kind, the same principles hold true for you when it comes to witnessing for Christ among your friends.

Decisions! Decisions! Decisions!

On what basis will you make yours?

You and Your Friends

13

ARE ALL YOUNG PEOPLE LIKE ME?

Oᴺᴇ ᴏᴜᴛꜱᴛᴀɴᴅɪɴɢ ᴛʀᴀɪᴛ about the U. S. college student is that he is not acting at all as a college student is supposed to" (Time, Nov. 18, 1957, *Education*).

How is a college student supposed to act? How is any young person supposed to act?

The old traditional theme is that college students are intellectuals and excited about philosophy and existentialism. The truth is that many college students do not know what the word "existentialism" means! They are not excited about philosophy and they are not intellectuals, *per se.*

College students are just like the teenagers that grow up in your father's home. That is, just like you and all the rest of the gang that went to high school together. That only a small percentage of high-schoolers go on to college does not mean that only the would-be "intellectuals" go on to higher education. And it does not mean that only the non-intellectual works! It means that only those whose parents have enough cash, or only those who have enough ambition to earn their own expenses make it to college. As I write this book 160,000 more students are in college than a year ago, and each coming year promises a bumper crop of freshmen, with our colleges running over onto long waiting lists.

College students are natural, normal Americans. They almost all dress alike. They all like to eat and to have fun. They all want to date. They all want letters and money from home . . . and food too, in boxes from mother.

A minister once asked me, "Aren't college students anti-religious? Agnostic? Aren't most of them unbelievers?"

Yes, most of them are unbelievers, but not total unbelievers. No, most of them are not agnostic (that is, confirmed doubters with antagonistic questions). Most young people are not anti-religious. Let's face the truth: they just have not yet met one single person who is able to communicate the love of Jesus Christ. They may have met many so-called "religious persons," but their great need is to meet Jesus Christ — in the life of just one person who totally believes in Him and loves Him, and who knows how to share Him.

"Not total unbelievers" means that many of them are "partial believers." Let me illustrate: Mina W. was sitting in her dormitory room one night with the door half open, when someone called up and down the halls, "Anyone for Bible study tonight? Room 220!" She went. She kept on going. She became a convinced believer. And now only eight months since her conversion, she is teaching a group of freshmen girls in that same dormitory once a week, and also once a week she is teaching a group of high school girls about Jesus Christ. I asked her what made her want to go to that first Bible study. "I didn't have any religious instruction at home, and while I believed in God, I didn't know *what* I believed about Him and this was the first real opportunity I had to find out."

So Mina is one of those students who has never rejected God, but who, while believing in all she did know, needed that personal touch from other students in order to know the Lord Jesus Christ as her own personal Saviour.

That story could be multiplied by hundreds.

Mollie was a high school student who had that personal touch for others because she loved Jesus Christ. One day she woke up to the fact that she was spending all her time with other Christians. In other words she was continually running to little "safety zones." Thinking it over, she knew what she could do and she did it. Each noon in the school cafeteria after her tray was filled, she deliberately passed by the table where the "Christians" sat, joined a group of "rebels" and spent her noon hour eating, talking, laughing and making friends with them. Her relaxed, natural behavior with them so impressed one of her high school teachers, that later the teacher, through a chain of circumstances which included reading "The Burden is Light" by Eugenia Price, came to see her need of Jesus Christ. Mollie's love for Christ took her *to* — not away from — young people like herself. This same teacher, who once had scoffed, became the enthusiastic sponsor of Mollie's Bible Club.

Jo Anne M. went forward at one of the Billy Graham campaigns and later attended a state teachers' college. A friend invited her to the Christian Fellowship group meeting on that campus. After that Jo Anne took her place among them and let others know she was a Christian. During her junior year, while attending an Inter-Varsity summer camp on Catalina Island, she came to talk with me one afternoon. "Ros, I don't think I really am a true believer. I know I went forward, but I didn't know much, and now I wonder if I'm a real Christian." I questioned her more closely on just why she thought that, and it finally boiled down to this: She had taken the necessary initial step at the Graham meeting, but Jesus Christ was not a reality in her life; she did things mostly because she was supposed to and because other Christians did them too. After that we had several quiet talks on the Person and the Work of Jesus Christ, and *why* it was necessary for Him to die, and the full meaning of the resurrection for her. Jo Anne was a partial believer, now she has become an active believer and knows Whom she believes.

Bobbi M. was president of her dormitory. She was popular, had a steady boy-friend, but had absolutely no religious background. She was not anti-religious and she was not even a "partial believer." She just did not seem to be interested. Her dates kept her busy, and all her extra-curricular activities pushed her studies aside, until she only averaged 5 or 6 hours sleep a night.

After she had accepted Jesus Christ as her Saviour, I asked her to tell me about how it happened.

"It was because of Ruby," she told me. "Once a week she came to my room to invite me to the Bible study in her room."

"Did you go?" I asked.

"Oh, about three times," Bobbi said.

Three times! I knew Ruby had been having those informal Bible studies about Jesus Christ for two years in her dormitory, and that between 40 and 50 girls had been contacted during that time.

"What happened? Why didn't you go oftener?" I asked.

"Went twice," said Bobbi, "and then I saw that the girls there — that is, most of them — knew more about the Bible and religion than I did." Shrugging her shoulders half defensively, she went on, "I didn't want anyone to know how ignorant I was, so I just stayed away."

Knowing Ruby, and her love and insistence which made girls feel wanted, I had another question.

"Didn't Ruby keep inviting you? What did you tell her? Did she know?"

"Yeah, she kept inviting me all right, and I kept telling her I was too busy. Why, one night when I told her that, she stamped her foot — you know Ruby — and said, 'Bobbi M., I'll never invite you again' and we both laughed. But she always did."

Through the faithfulness and love of one girl in that dormitory, more than 20 girls have come to know Jesus Christ personally. These girls were not hard to reach. No one had tried until Ruby came. Once a week, from 10:30 p.m. until 11:00 p.m. in her room, Ruby took simple paragraphs from the life of the Lord Jesus, showing that He was God in the flesh and that He loved people like herself. Most of them "put their hair up" during that time. Everything was informal, the little Bible study, what the girls wore, the discussion, and the atmosphere.

In most of the nation's colleges and high schools, students don't want to be different. They want to know what other students think. "I want to know what others believe, because I want something to believe in myself," one student told me.

Yes, other students are a great deal like you. Full

of life, wanting thrills, wanting dates, wanting to be popular, and not wanting to "hit the books" too hard, but
enough to get decent grades.

And then there is God. If you don't know anything
about Him, but want to, you will find friends to help you.
If you know something, but want to know more — you will
find Christian friends among the students who want to
meet you and share with you. If you do know God, through
and in the Person of the Lord Jesus Christ, You will be the
connecting link between Him and that student with an open
mind and a hungry heart who wants to know.

If you are on familiar, sure ground with Jesus
Christ, you need not feel "strange" with other students.
After all, they are, at heart, just "people" like you. And
remember these are THE YEARS THAT COUNT.

14

HOW DIFFERENT SHOULD
A CHRISTIAN BE?

LET ME ASK YOU ONE FIRST. Do you like to be different? No, no one wants to be different because being different usually means not being accepted. And not being accepted means being alone. And loneliness is tragedy!

Here's another question. Just how different was Jesus of Nazareth from other men who walked the streets of Capernaum? What made Him different? Could people tell by looking at the way He dressed, the places He went, His associates, His language — could they tell by these things *who He was*? Or did they have to be with Him first, and listen to what He taught, and observe the things He did, the way He conducted Himself?

Our Lord was known to be a friend of sinners. How many friends do you have among the unbelievers on your campus? Do they know you as their friend? Or, do you shun them, so that they have no way of knowing how you conduct yourself and what you believe?

Yes, I know these are hard things to face. Especially because during your growing-up days in high school, it seemed the thing to do to be like the kids in your group; you thought and talked and dressed very much alike. But you are a Christian, and this applies to you whether you are in high school or college, whether you are holding a job or teaching school, whether you are married or unmarried, male or female. You are a servant and follower of Jesus Christ and He has put you where you are to be His witnesses.

Just how different should you be? And should your "difference" make non-Christians aware that they are "different" too? Should your difference set you apart so that you are obviously *different?*

Have you ever heard anyone pray like this? "Lord bless us this day and help us so that others will know we are different and want what we have." You have probably prayed like that yourself. I did before I really thought this through in the Presence of the Saviour who loves sinners in a way that always surprises me. I confess, I don't have this kind of love except as He gives it to me. But He wants to give it to me and *does* when I take it. Do we want them to know we are different, or do we want them to know Christ?

I remember visiting two freshmen girls in a State College who had prayed that they would find Christian roommates. They did. Then one of them said, "Ros, I've already witnessed to all the girls on this wing of the dorm!"

"You have!" I was pleased and surprised because it was only two weeks since classes started. "What did you tell them?"

"They all know exactly where I stand in regard to worldly things. I told them I didn't dance, I didn't play cards, I didn't go to shows, and I didn't wear lipstick and I didn't smoke. They all know I'm different and that I'm a Christian."

I thought a minute.

"Well, Nan, now I suppose they all want to be like you?"

She looked down.

"You don't want them to be like *you*. Do you? You really want them to be like Jesus Christ, don't you?"

"Oh, Ros, I never thought of it like that. I *was* talking about myself, wasn't I? Oh, what'll I do now?"

We both considered. Finally I said, "Well, one thing you could do is go out and buy some lipstick, go into the dressing room when they are all there and ask them to help you put it on. And all the while, if I were you, I'd be praying that someone would say, 'Why, Nan, I thought you didn't wear lipstick!' Then you could say, 'Lipstick is beside the point. What I said to you the other day about the things I *don't* do, is *not* the point. I've begun to think through what I really believe. I'm sorry about all that negative-attitude stuff. That isn't Christianity. Christianity is Jesus Christ. Outward things are not nearly as important as inward things, I've found out. Belonging to Him is what counts. I hope you girls understand. I'd like to be friends.'"

Nan hid her face in her hands. "Oh, Ros, I *never* could do that! But what *will* I do?" We agreed that we would just keep praying and the Lord Himself would show her what to do.

Nan and her roommate avoided me for some months, but I understood. Then she came to summer camp and right into my cabin, and she was wearing a touch of lipstick. With much relief she said, "What a struggle I've had! My Christianity was all, do this and don't do that. Keeping rules, trying to measure up to what others thought of me. I really did accept Christ as my Saviour, but it seems I just looked at outward things and I judged others by those things too. I'm just beginning to understand what you mean when you say, 'Christianity is a Person' and that is why I'm here for more help. Ros, what's lipstick compared to being a witness? I had myself shut off from the very girls who needed Him!"

That story has a good ending. Nan went to another University to be a real witness for Christ. She's living in a house with Jewish girls and God is using her there. The Lord has used her also to help other Christians re-think what Christianity really is.

How different should a Christian be?

"Look at that bunch of girls over there! They are Christians. Don't make friends with them, or you'll be looking like them!" This was actually said by one girl who later understood that being a Christian meant believing on the Person of Jesus Christ, receiving His life *within,* and being changed from *within.* Yes, there are changes both inwardly and outwardly, but they should not keep you from being friends with sinners. If your outward appearance and dress do not attract more attention than your inner life, you are all right.

Dr. Robert Smith, professor of Philosophy at Bethel College, points out four areas of life which *should* be radically changed because one is trusting Christ as Saviour and obeying Him as Lord.

1. *Time.* How do you use your time? Work time, study time, spare time?

2. *Sex.* Is Jesus Christ Lord in your sex life? Does He have something to say to you and do you follow Him?

3. *Yourself.* The right to do as you please. The

right to be yourself. A follower of Christ has no personal
rights.

4. *Money.* However little you may have now, some
day you will have more. Is Christ Lord here? Do you
consult with Him about what you have, what you give, how
you spend it, how you get it?

A true believer in Jesus Christ will be known by his
inner reactions and obedience in these four areas and in
many others as well. This is where the real difference
shows up. We should remember, "Man looketh on the
outward appearance, but the Lord looketh on the heart."

If you want others to know that there is a "difference"
between you and them, it will, of course, take more than
"silent living" although I do most emphatically believe
that *living the life* is of top importance. But notice I said,
it will take *more* than that. It will take faith and courage
and conviction on your part that JESUS CHRIST MAKES THE
DIFFERENCE, so that you will begin to tell them about Him
too. They need to be told. But you must *win* a hearing.
People want to know about Jesus Christ, as He really is.
He Himself is the "good news." And He said,

"Ye shall be witnesses unto ME" (not unto your
Christian selves!).

15

WHAT ABOUT DATING?

R—— RING! R—— RING! The telephone on second floor Crawford Hall was insistent. Suddenly the whole floor of girls was quiet. Waiting. Then the announcement came. This time it was not a call for a certain girl. It was —

"Two girls for a blind date! Who wants to go?"

"Does that happen very often here?" I asked Kay W.

"Oh, yes, all the time," she replied.

"Who goes?"

"You'd be surprised. Girls want dates you know. Your popularity is measured by the dates you get."

"What about the Christian fellows — do they date?"

"W —— ell," she hesitated, "not very much. And sometimes they date non-Christian girls instead of Christian girls. Why I know a swell Christian girl who never had one date all the time she was in college — and look at the Christian fellows around this place."

One young man said to me, "The Christian witness on our campus suffers greatly because of the problems connected with Christians' dating." He went on to say that students either do not date at all or they get carried away too far, which raises more problems.

Problems! Problems! How can we do something about them? The best way is to face them and begin to talk about them.

One evening after a hay-ride, I saw three college fellows in a corner and thought it might be a good time to pick up some information.

I plunged right in, "Why do so few Christian fellows date?"

"That's easy," said one of them. "No money. No girl."

"Aw — Tom, there are plenty of things going on right on campus where you don't need money," said Al.

I tried again. "Give me an answer. I'm serious."

"I'll tell you why I don't date," the silent fellow spoke up. "Most Christian girls can't carry on a decent, intelligent conversation on any current subject. What's a fellow going to do? Ya gotta talk! And they can't. That's why I stopped dating."

Tom spoke up again. "Yeah, ya got something there all right. Another thing," he turned to me, "most Christian girls don't know how to dress, or do their hair. Why don't they fix themselves up so a fellow will be proud to be seen with them?"

Well, why don't they?

Now let's get down to facts. There are two subjects which need airing. One is dating and the other is marriage. I believe that if we can see what God has planned as the end-result, we will be able to face both with more objectivity and more common sense.

Marriage

Girls, here are a few questions to ask yourselves very early before your undependable emotions get you tied into knots.

Does the fellow you like love Jesus Christ?

Would you be proud of him as the head of your home and the father of your children?

Could he take the spiritual lead in your home?

Does he take the lead now in your relationship with him?

(Read Ephesians 5:17-33 which is very important.)

What do other fellows think about him?

Does he get along well in a group?

Would he fit into the social life of your family, or would you be embarrassed to take him home to meet your parents?

What, specifically, do you have in common?

Can you quietly discuss something about which you do not agree?

Can you pray aloud and meet the Lord together?

Fellows, you should ask the same basic questions about that girl who is so attractive to you.

Does she love Jesus Christ?

Would you be proud of her as the mother of your children?

Would you be proud to introduce her to your parents?

Does she understand you, and is she interested in you or in herself?

What are your common interests?

Can you discuss things without arguing?

Can you meet the Lord in prayer together?

What do other girls think about her?

Now, we have not covered the field by any means. We have only tried to point up the spiritual side of it, with a few questions which have been helpful to other students. But let these questions at least begin to stimulate your thinking at an early stage in your dating.

The Bible teaches that a woman's first calling is at the side of her husband. Even before the mission field, or Christian service, I feel a young woman should seriously consider the marriage offer from a sincere Christian man. This is God's normal plan. If He wants that girl on the mission field she will get there — with her husband — in God's own time and will.

Of course, if marriage is not offered that's a different matter. She should move ahead in preparation toward God's place for her. Several couples have told me that they met each other only after they had given themselves wholly to God to live alone for Him if He willed.

But remember, marriage is not everything.

One of God's greatest missionary saints (a single woman) is quoted as having said, "After all, marriage is one circumstance of the Christian life. Being single is another." Think that over. Its implications are deep!

CHRISTIAN DATING

Now let's get back to dating.

Dating is an important institution, since this is where marriage usually starts. Telephone calls, dressing up, meeting, going out together, getting acquainted, sharing experiences. Full moon! Fun! Love! If God is in them, these experiences should be the happiest of all your days. They should be and they can be.

Dating by two's is not necessarily a sound idea. It

puts the couple in a difficult position in many ways. There is the emotional strain of trying to be at one's best and feeling socially inadequate. There are the inevitable questions, "Should I go out with her again?" "Is he the right one?" "How can I know for sure?" "How do others find out?"

Did you ever hear of the "brother-sister relationship"? Before you brand me as a stuffy "older woman," let me illustrate.

Inter-Varsity Christian Fellowship has a month-long summer training camp on Catalina Island in California. One year at the end of the first ten days, tension had already begun because couples wanted to date and there was "no dating" on our island! We finally had an open meeting with all present and talked about everything together. Then the boys knew what to expect, and so did the girls. We suggested a good wholesome brother-sister relationship. That is, doing things in groups, not pairs; of eating together at meals and finding out about everyone at the table, instead of pairing off; or washing dishes, doing camp work, camp studies together — in groups. Get acquainted as Christian brothers and sisters and forget about trying to fall in love.

It worked! The tension dropped. Everyone relaxed and had a wonderful time, and got genuinely acquainted. Someone said, "Why don't we do this back on campus? We'd get to know each other as real people."

A young man who just graduated from college had said good-by to his friends in the Christian Fellowship (whom he had known for four years) and was driving home for the last time. He said to himself, "Oh, how I am going to miss that gang, and all the good times we had together, and all the things we did together." Suddenly another thought occurred to him. " —— miss that gang? The one I am really going to miss is Helen! Why, come to think of it, even though we've never had a date, I've never met a girl like her." The sudden idea so gripped him, that he pulled over to the curb and stopped his car. "Say," he said to himself, "why don't you marry that girl? You know all about her, and you'll never find another one like her. She's just the one you've been looking for, you idiot. Get going, boy!" Bob and Helen were married and lived happily ever afterward. They really had come to know each other through the activities of the fellowship group on that campus.

This kind of "gang fun" or "group working together" can be built up and made to provide for natural relaxed relationships between young people right in your own town, or your own church, or your own home. You may need a young married couple to help you, to provide a home and facilities for food, but it can be done. There are many kinds of fun and many kinds of work you can do together. The important thing is not to rush into an engagement before you really know each other.

After all, fellows, there's really no big rush. As my friend Art Glasser says, "Adam didn't run around looking for Eve. God sent her to him!"

For further reading: *Toward Christian Marriage,* by Capper and Williams (Inter-Varsity Press). *Life and Love,* by Clyde Narramore (Zondervan).

16

WHAT ABOUT DATING
NON-CHRISTIANS?

WHAT ABOUT CHRISTIANS dating non-Christians?

We might as well get into this subject, because everywhere I go, I find girls asking me this question. Girls seem to have more trouble with this than fellows. Not that fellows don't date non-Christians. They do. But girls seem to be more aware of the problem involved. When one dates a non-Christian, there is always the possibility of love and marriage.

A university girl approached a counsellor about this matter. She said, "I'd like to have you pray that our marriage will work out. Gerry is not a Christian, but we love each other."

The staff member went right to the painful point. "I'm sorry, but I can't pray about your marriage. Because the Bible plainly states that a believer should not marry an unbeliever" (see II Cor. 6:14-18). Then she added, "Now it is right for us to pray that Gerry will become a believer, but we have to keep our motives clear. First, that he will become a believer, and not that he will become a believer so you can marry him. Do you think you can let God straighten out your motives, so He can get through to Gerry's heart?"

Falling in love is a major event in the life of any young person. All other interests seem secondary. In fact, all other interests seem to bend and bow to "the loved one" until after marriage, when the normal routine begins again, and then differences of opinion surprisingly assert themselves with much strength and sometimes stubbornness.

When I was eighteen years old, I was planning to go to China as a missionary, and a young man who professed to love me announced loudly that he, too, was called to China! Fortunately, I found out that his "call to China as a missionary" was wholly linked to his so-called love for me. He didn't get to China, and he didn't get me! But I look back now on thirteen wonderful years spent in China in God's will.

Falling in love can blind one to many things, especially things of a spiritual nature which have to do with God . . . *if* the other person has not a personal knowledge of Jesus Christ and a deep willingness to be led by His Spirit.

I know of many instances where girls have married fellows who are not believers, and whom they began to date because there seemed to be no Christian fellows around at the time. One girl told me that Harry wanted to become a believer and was on the way. They have been married four years now, have a baby boy, and Harry has never held anything steadily but a bottle. The girl has stopped going to church almost altogether.

Do you really want God's will in regard to your boy-friend? Do you really want God's will in regard to your marriage? Then you must start with that *first date,* for one date leads to another, and can eventually lead you to the marriage altar. You can't predict when you'll fall in love. A young man who fell in love after his fourth date, remarked, "It sure was a good thing Mary Alice was a Christian, wasn't it?" Stop and think before you get on the emotional slide and cannot get off.

Yes, I believe that God knows your future. I believe you can pray, "Lord, lead me to the right one, and prepare me now by the experiences I am going through so I will know how to live with people and do Your will at the same time."

But let's get back to dating non-Christians. Girls just will date non-Christians. Why? Because there is usually a shortage of keen Christian fellows, and the non-Christian may be a nice, good-looking boy and after all — "a girl has to date once in a while, doesn't she?"

If you are one who feels you can get away with it, and enjoy your evening, enjoy yourself, and enjoy your date — read this story about Janice. I'm not saying every girl could do the same thing, but at least it could give you some ideas.

Janice B. who loves Jesus Christ is an attractive brunette in a large university. At every important dress or sports function on campus, one can find Janice with a non-Christian fellow from some popular fraternity. I asked her once if she thought there might be a possibility of falling in love with one of them.

"I don't even think about that, Ros. I just thank God that I have the opportunity to talk about Jesus Christ to these fellows. More than ever, *I know* that the man I marry must absolutely belong to Jesus Christ. I don't want any other. It wouldn't work anyway."

Talking further to her, I found that early in the evening she brings up the subject of religion, for she has found that it is easier to talk to fellows about religion than almost any other subject.

The secret of her popularity is that she is not only attractive to look at, she is interesting to talk to, and she knows how to listen. For a good-looking girl like Janice to be a convinced believer, and to have such an interesting approach, simply takes the fellows off-guard, and they find themselves interested. "Talking religion" to Janice means finding out what her escort believes about the Person of Jesus Christ and whether he has considered the fact that Jesus is the God of this universe and that He invaded Earth in the form of Man.

Again I say, you may not be able to do what Janice does. Not many Christian young people can survive this dating problem. There is always the temptation to carry it farther and farther, and to fall in love, even though the person dated is not a Christian. Janice constantly kept herself aware that it could wind up in more than she had bargained for. If you find that you cannot turn the conversation to Jesus Christ, and discover what he or she believes on that first or second date (while you are still emotionally uninvolved) you will probably never be able to find out. Because your unpredictable heart will keep on taking more and more control of the situation. You'd better play safe and stop dating that non-Christian fellow or girl, for there is the potential of enough pain and agony in love between Christians without adding a "broken heart" because you are out of God's will in your love.

If you really want to know if your date is serious or not, after you have had several conversations, here is a good way to find out. Ask some older Christian friend, preferably another fellow, to meet your boy-friend, and have a talk with him about being a Christian, or about Christianity. A fellow can fool his girl-friend, but he can't fool another fellow!

Then there is the story of Alice H. who had already become engaged to Harry, a non-Christian who had promised her again and again that he would accept Jesus Christ. But he kept putting it off.

One morning as Alice was having her daily Quiet Time, she seemed to hear the Lord's voice in her heart, "You are *My child*. How can you belong to one who does not belong to Me?" With tears, but determined to obey, Alice told Harry she couldn't marry him.

"I always intended to become a Christian," Harry said, as he told me the story, "but maybe I never would have, if I hadn't been shocked into it because Alice obeyed the Lord that morning."

You've heard it before. Hear it again. You cannot reform a man after you marry him. Yes, there are exceptions to every rule and there are fellows who become believers after marriage, but the sorrow and the heartache and the clash of opinions and ways of living and thinking will bring you much suffering. Our Lord is able to hear and answer your prayers. Your part is to obey Him and let Him work in that man's heart without any hindrance from you. Your part is to love and obey Jesus Christ and He will bring all good things to you in His own time.

Friendship and love can be based happily on sound Biblical principles of obedience to Christ. Don't get the idea that God is trying to make life difficult for you in the love-department! After all, God is love and He is all for it. He is the best marriage counsellor. It may seem for a time that He is being unreasonable, but just be patient and wait. What He is trying to do is to clarify things for you, and put you in touch with the person He may have chosen for you.

God knows the future. If you take His Word for things now, you'll find you will be much happier during those years ahead when the honeymoon is over.

And all these things go for fellows too!

For another story about dating non-Christians see next chapter, "What Is 'Christian Fellowship'?"

17

WHAT IS "CHRISTIAN FELLOWSHIP"?

L ET'S GET TOGETHER AFTER CHURCH for some Christian fellowship," said the youth director. So they did. They sang some choruses to pep everyone up, served refreshments, told a few jokes, played a few games, said a goodnight prayer, and went home. What he might have said was, "Let's get together after church and enjoy one another's company." For that is what they actually did. This is fellowship among Christians, but strictly speaking it is not "Christian fellowship."

What is Christian fellowship?

Joan L. found out for herself as she read her Bible and participated in group fellowship. You can read what she discovered for yourself in I John 1:1-3. But this is the story.

When there was a fellowship meeting announced, Joan was there. She loved to sing and pray and share what Jesus Christ was coming to mean in her own life.

The young people sat informally in a circle, recognizing first of all that they were there to meet Christ in the special way He had indicated, since He had promised that, "where two or three have gathered in My name, I am there with them" (Matt. 18:20 — Berkeley Version).

104

They began by singing hymns of praise to His Name. They offered simple, short prayers of thanksgiving for His Love, His Power and His Presence in their lives. They gave thanks for who He was, the Lord God, their Saviour and Redeemer.

Then they shared with one another the varying ways in which they had found Christ to be real and present during the time since they had last met. Someone told how it was made possible for him to love a person who had greatly wronged him. Another told how prayer for his parents had been answered. Another explained how he had been able to speak of Christ to his roommate.

Then there was a time to pray aloud together. We'll go into that a bit later on in this chapter, because prayer is an important part of Christian fellowship for young people.

This all seems so good, what else could Joan find out about Christian fellowship? What was missing?

She came to me one day with her New Testament already opened to I John 1:1-3. "I can scarcely wait to tell you what I found! Listen: 'That which we have seen and heard declare we unto you, that ye also may have fellowship with us: and truly our fellowship is with the Father, and with his son Jesus Christ'" (I John 1:3). Her eyes were shining as she told me more of her exciting discovery.

"I always thought that having 'Christian fellowship' meant just to pray and sing and share with one another. But I was forever trying to 'pump up' something within me, or to get my inspiration from the people around me. Sometimes it worked and sometimes it didn't. What I've finally seen in these verses, is that *first* I must have living fellowship with Jesus Christ. I must 'see' Him, 'hear' Him, and tell others about Him, and *then* fellowship with those who love Him will just naturally follow."

In other words, Joan had found out what we all need to discover: that fellowship begins with the vertical relationship with our Lord Himself, and then there will be reality in the horizontal relationships with our fellow-believers. We don't have to "whip up" anything, or try to "pep up" our Christian fellowship. The presence of the Holy Spirit will be in the midst of believers who are in constant touch with the Lord and Christian growth and maturity will be the natural results.

Christian fellowship is enjoying the Presence of our Lord Jesus Christ, rejoicing together because of Him, sharing His burdens *and* ours, and praying for one another.

It is in the midst of this kind of living fellowship with believers that young people begin to grow and mature.

If the desire is in your heart to be a part of such a living fellowship centered in Jesus Christ, He will lead you to another Christian and as the two of you pray together, you will be led by His Spirit to others who will join you. Life reproduces itself. Jesus said, "I if I be lifted up will draw all men unto me."

Let me tell you how two girls started such a Christian fellowship in their dormitory.

Karen O. stopped me as I was walking through Wilmer Hall. "Don't I know you?" she asked. We finally decided we had met at a Young Life Retreat a year ago. Immediately, she pulled me to one side and said, "I've got a problem. I'm going with a swell fellow, but he is not a Christian. What am I going to do? I really love him too."

My first question was, "Have you told him you are a Christian?"

Karen was embarrassed because she hadn't told him, and moreover, she had not been faithful in her own Christian life. Matthew 18:19, 20 came to my mind.

"Do you know another Christian girl in this dorm?"

"Ye — es, I know Jan. She lives right down the hall."

I knew her, too, and knew she loved Jesus Christ. We knocked at her door and went in.

"Jan, Karen is concerned about her boy-friend, Chuck. He isn't a Christian. I believe that Jesus Christ meant what he said in Matthew 18:19, 20." We opened the Bible and read it.

"Once more I assure you that if two of you are agreed on earth about anything for which you pray, it will be done for you by My heavenly Father. For where two or three have gathered in My name, I am there with them" (Berkeley Version).

After we talked awhile, this is what the girls decided to do:

1. To meet for five minutes every night right after supper to pray together that their own faith might be strengthened and that Chuck might become a believer in Jesus Christ.

2. That instead of each praying a long prayer, they would have "conversational prayer," that is, recognizing the Presence of the Lord Jesus with them, they would speak to Him as though He actually were present and they were conversing with Him and with each other. Instead of one prayer, they would pray back and forth, each

one perhaps five or six times, as it seemed necessary by the urgency in their hearts.

3. That they would pray simple, short honest prayers in their own words, using "I" when they meant themselves, and "we" when they both were agreed.

4. That they would pray "faith-sized requests." That is, they would ask for those things which they believed God could grant within 24 hours, which meant the next time they met for prayer.

"What could the first faith-sized request be?" they wanted to know. I suggested we pray right then, and that the Holy Spirit who is faithful would put it into our hearts. We did . . . and the request came up . . . and we all believed it could be done within 24 hours!

It was this: That the Lord would give Karen courage to tell Chuck that she was a Christian that night when she met him for their date after study-hours.

I had to leave their campus the next day and move on to another college. But two weeks later I was back. Both girls poured out the exciting story of answered prayer.

That night Karen had gone out to tell Chuck that she was a Christian. But she could not quite make it. Her hands got cold and wet, and her tongue became like a piece of wood. So the next night Jan and Karen prayed the same prayer. Karen came back into the dormitory floating on clouds! Not only did she tell him, but he was interested, wanted to know how it happened, and wanted to know about being a Christian. He had little religious background and did not come from a Christian family.

So the requests went on, night after night. They prayed that he would be willing to read the New Testament. He was. They prayed that he would attend the weekly Christian meeting on campus. He said he would. They prayed that the speaker would present Jesus Christ and not give some vague talk. He did. They prayed for me, as I spoke the next week, and they prayed that Chuck would give his heart to Jesus Christ *that night*. He did.

About four weeks later when I visited that campus, instead of the original two there was a roomful of girls meeting at 6:45 A.M. for 30 minutes of prayer. Jan had just come from a visit home. Her "faith-sized request" had been that she might be able to pray with her mother. Her report was so good, and the relationship with her mother so real, that other girls began to pray that the same thing might take place on their next visit home. Young believers had grown spiritually, partial-believers had come out openly and declared their faith, strong personal testimonies were going out to friends on campus, and through letters, to friends off campus. *And* more boy-friends had received Jesus Christ as Lord and Saviour.

As you have read this chapter, you may be saying to yourself, "I wish I knew a group of people like that. I wish I could belong to a fellowship group like that." This longing is in the heart of every true child of God, and in the hearts of many who are wanting to be His children. You can be part of such a group. Right in your own high school Bible Club, right in your own church, right in your own town, right in your own home.

"How can I do this?" you ask. Just as Karen and Jan started with a need *too big* for them. Then they began to pray together, to ask "faith-sized requests," to pray honestly and simply. You too can start with that need which is *too big* for you, and with just one friend.

"Who will that friend be? I don't know anyone."

Well, this one thing I do know: since the Holy Spirit is giving you a longing for this kind of fellowship, He will certainly guide you to the person who will be your first partner. You don't have to convince your whole group that this is a good idea. Fellowship like this starts with two people who are convinced that the risen Lord Jesus is there with you to answer that need which is too big for you. Don't get me wrong. This is not a "come-outer group" idea. This is a "strengthening-the-group-from-within" idea. Living things grow because they are alive.

> Yes, the Life has been revealed and we have seen and are witnessing and are announcing to you the Life Eternal, who existed with the Father and has been revealed to us. We saw Him and we heard Him and are telling you, so you too may have [enjoy] fellowship along with us. And this fellowship of ours is with the Father and with His Son Jesus Christ. This we are writing you so that your joy may be complete.
> (I John 1:2, 3 — Berkeley Version).

You and God

18

AM I A CHRISTIAN?

We have come to the last chapter in THE YEARS THAT COUNT. It could be the first chapter in your Life. Life written with a capital "L," because it will be the year that counts most in your whole life, because you discovered what being a Christian really means.

"A Christian is one who is responding to Jesus Christ," wrote Mr. Simpson, in *The Fact of Christ,* one of the clearest books I can recommend for a person who wants to be both intellectually and emotionally convinced.

Notice I said, "for a person who *wants* to be — convinced." Until God draws you like a magnet draws steel, you will never *want* Jesus Christ. When He begins to draw you to Himself, there is a lessening of the natural resistance within you. "No man can come to me, except the Father which hath sent me draw him" (John 6:44). And "All that the Father giveth me shall come to me; and him that cometh to me I will in no wise cast out" (John 6:37).

It is my belief that the unwise methods often used by over-zealous believers who want to force a quick decision, result in distorted ideas of God, of His love, and of His ways with so-called agnostics, or undecided believers.

His eternal love is stronger than the law of gravity, and His pull is *just* as powerful, and who would want to get away from the love which has given itself on a Cross?

You can get away from the unwelcome person or the radio program that rubs you the wrong way, but God's love goes right with you, wooing you and waiting for you. Yes, God waits for you. He is waiting for you now.

But how does one become a Christian?

I'd like to give you several simple explanations. I've used all kinds of verses and methods and outlines, and I have seen girls and fellows come to know Jesus Christ as their own Saviour under so many circumstances, that I know now that it isn't *how* I say it, or *what* I say, the big factor is *God's drawing your heart, and your response to Him.*

We can begin with two simple things.

1. If you are even beginning to respond to Jesus Christ in your own heart, there is evidence that God is drawing you and that Faith has begun to spring up. Faith is a gift to you from God (Eph. 2:8, 9). You don't have to go around pumping it up. You don't have to depend upon someone else to assure you. Acknowledge to yourself that you are responding. Acknowledge to Him that you are responding.

2. Let this acknowledgment take the form of gratitude which actually gives thanks. Speak to Him, He is there. That's how simple it is. No gift is completely possessed until there is an acknowledgment and a giving of thanks. Jesus Christ is Eternal Life (John 17:3). This means, He is the gift and with Him will eventually come everything else you need — in this life and in the next.

If these seem too simple for you, let's try another

approach which has worked for hundreds of young people also. The original idea of the ABC's of becoming a Christian I heard from the Reverend Mr. Stott of London, while he was giving a series of evangelistic lectures to the students at the University of British Columbia. I am not sure he would recognize them as they are stated here. But using his main outline, I have adapted it to your needs in order that the experience of becoming a Christian might be centered in the Person of Christ, rather than in a subjective "experience" of what might be taking place in you.

Here is the outline:

  A. Something to Admit.
  B. Something to Believe.
  C. Something to Consider.
  D. Something to Do.

A. *Something to Admit.* We have already said that unless you *want* Christ, He will wait until you do want Him. What is it that needs to be admitted? Your need of Him. Your incompleteness without Him. Your need of a Saviour. Your having left Him out of your life so long. Jesus Himself said in John 16:7-11 (especially in the ninth verse) that sin is simply not believing in Him. No matter what else you may feel about yourself, and your past, *this* is the subject which is important. Have you admitted your need of Jesus Christ as your *personal* Saviour?

B. *Something to Believe.* What does one have to believe? How much does one have to believe in order to become a Christian? It would be a good thing for you to get a New Testament and read these verses — John 3:16; 1:12; 17:3; 20:31. "God so loved the world that He gave His only begotten Son . . ." that means He gave a part of Himself to die on the Cross . . . for you. Do you believe that Jesus Christ is "God-with-us"? Read also John 1:1-14. Believing on His Name means knowing who He is. How can you believe? Remember that the basis of faith is fact. Fact then demands a decision. Jesus Christ is an historical Person who both by indirect and direct claims in all He said and did, reveals to all who are ready, that He is GOD IN THE FLESH. Do you believe this? (Read also Matthew 1:21, 22, 23.)

C. *Something to Consider.* You consider the cost. What does it cost to be a Christian? It cost Jesus Christ everything. It will cost you everything, too. Read Mark 8:34. "Whosoever will come after me, let him deny himself, and take up his cross, and follow me." You accept Him as Saviour, when you admit your need of Him. But you also must consider that Jesus Christ is LORD. His name is, the *Lord* Jesus Christ. What does this mean? This means He wants not only your heart but your life too. It means He wants to be the loving Lord who will direct and guide you. But to do this, you must give yourself to Him, willingly. You have not only received "forgiveness," you have received "the Forgiver" and along with Him everything you need will be given to you. He is the Lord. I remember John Stott saying, "Consider what it costs to give up yourself. There are too many hypocrites in the church already. I'm not interested in bringing in any more."

And with your *considering,* remember "love controls" and read II Corinthians 5:14, 15. The cost is not giving up "things" it is *giving up yourself.* It is acting as though Jesus Christ is Lord.

D. *Something to Do.* What else could there be to do? You have already done several things: A. You have admitted your need of Jesus Christ as your Saviour. B. You

have stated your belief in His Name and in the fact that He
is God, the God who died for you and walked out of that
tomb alive, and who lives forevermore! C. You have considered the cost of receiving Jesus Christ as Lord and
Saviour of your life.

What else is there to do?

Only one thing: *To give thanks* to Him for all that
He has done, *to give thanks* to Him for the free gift of
Himself to you, *to give thanks* to Him for the gift of Life
forever with Him. In short: Give thanks for JESUS CHRIST.
Or, to put it another way, Give thanks *to* Jesus Christ.
I'm sure you have seen Warner Sallman's picture of Revelation 3:20. Christ is standing outside the door of your
heart. He has just knocked and His head is bent in a listen-
ing attitude for *your* word of welcome and *your* word of
response.

Christ is alive! He is living today. Something to
do? Yes, there is something to do — speak to Him, speak
with Him, voice your gratitude, your belief, your thanks.
The Giver is more important than all His gifts. Talk with
Him just as you would any other person, simply and honestly.

"Thank you, Lord Jesus Christ, for opening my eyes
to know who You are. I worship you as My Lord and My
God. Thank You for becoming my Saviour and thank You
for being my Lord. *Thank You for dying on the Cross
for me.* Thank You for the forgiveness of all my sins.
Thank You for loving me as I am. And thank You for
coming to live in my heart. Thank You! Thank You!
Thank You!"

A follow-up you, yourself, can use:

1. The chapters of this book re-read should now give

you help and direction. See "Should I Live for Now for the Future?" for help in your daily devotional time.

2. Be sure to purchase one or more of the newer translations of the New Testament, and read the gospels carefully to strengthen your awareness of Jesus Christ as God-in-the-flesh.

3. Read the Psalms in the Old Testament as expressions of your heart, in prayer, in petition, in thanksgiving. (When you come to the portions regarding "enemies" think of them as "forces of evil" which were against Jesus Christ and which He conquered.)

4. Very important for you is the chapter on "What Is 'Christian Fellowship'?" Pray that you may find such a group of Christians for it is in this atmosphere of faith and prayer that you will grow into a mature believer.

5. Finally, let your Christian life be truly Christ-centered, by exposing your heart to Jesus Christ Himself. "Thou shalt love the Lord thy God with all thy heart, and with all thy soul, and with all thy mind, and with all thy strength: this is the first commandment. And the second is like, namely this, Thou shalt love thy neighbour as thyself" (Mark 12:30, 31).

❖ ❖ ❖ ❖ ❖ ❖ ❖ ❖

We began this book by saying that *you* are important. You see, it is all right to love yourself. Jesus said it was. "Thou shalt love thy neighbor *as thyself.*" This kind of love works toward those around you, toward you and toward God, as long as it is "centered-down" in the Person of Jesus Christ. Love yourself, but be certain that your "self" is *in Him.* And be certain *now,* during THE YEARS THAT COUNT.